Voluntary Victims

Racism, Sexism, Heightism, and Avoiding the Big Victim on Campus Club

LESLIE BINGHAM

outskirts
press

Foreword

A coworker approached me and said, "Tell me what you hear."

From his cell phone a ridiculous, tinny, robotic voice repeated the word *yelly* several times.

"Yelly," I said.

"Huh?"

"What's 'yelly'?"

"You're fucking with me."

"What are you talking about?"

"It's *laurel*."

"Are you stoned right now?"

So was my introduction to the great Yanny vs. Laurel debate of 2018.

The robotic voice was saying "laurel," but depending on the pitch or tone or frequency or whatever science says is the case, it can sound different to some people. According to Twitter data, 47 percent of people heard "yanny."[1]

---

1   "Here's why you're hearing 'Yanny' — and why it's technically 'Laurel,'" *CBS News,* May 17, 2018, https://www.cbsnews.com/news/yanny-vs-laurel-debate-sparks-internet-controversy/

My hearing is more wrong than normal because I couldn't even hear that. Even though I know what I heard was wrong, I know what I heard.

This was like the Great Dress Debate of 2015, when a woman posted a picture on Tumblr and the nation was divided on whether the dress was blue and black or white and gold.[2]

These concepts have real-life consequences. For instance, scientists say eyewitness testimony isn't as reliable as most people think, yet jurors rely heavily on it to determine the fate of their fellow citizens.[3]

If we can't always trust what we think we see or hear, what other areas of life could we be woefully wrong about?

America is, now more than ever, a politically divided nation. It's partly due to stereotyping people based on who they voted for and projecting our own negative sensibilities onto those we disagree with. Be honest with yourself: when was the last time you imputed positive intent to a political enemy?

Since Donald Trump became president, the political rhetoric has amped up, and there's a huge swath of the population that believes Trump supporters are racist, misogynistic, and homophobic.

I'm not just talking about some random dude in his San Francisco bubble who has never met a conservative in his life. I'm talking high-profile individuals like MSNBC's Joe Scarborough, who said on his *Morning Joe* show in the summer of 2018, "[Trump supporters] cannot say, 'Oh, I'm just supporting him because he's giving them hell in Washington, D.C.' No, he's been openly racist, just like we said back in December

---

2   Dana Ford, "What color is this dress?" *CNN*, February 27, 2015, https://www.cnn.com/2015/02/26/us/blue-black-white-gold-dress/index.html
3   Hal Arkowitz and Scott O. Lilienfeld, "Why Science Tells Us Not to Rely on Eyewitness Accounts," *Scientific American*, January 1, 2010, https://www.scientificamerican.com/article/do-the-eyes-have-it/

of 2015, openly racist. If you support him, then you're supporting that, and you are that. It's that simple. That's what we've come to now."[4]

He's not alone. This sentiment is common among prominent guests on MSNBC and CNN.[5] They lack the ability to see it any other way.

We all project our own sensibilities onto others. Whether or not we're accurate is the issue at hand.

For example, Roseanne Barr tweeted in May 2018, "muslim brotherhood & planet of the apes had a baby = vj." The "vj" referred to ex-Obama advisor Valerie Jarrett, who is half black. I had a discussion with an avid liberal friend about the tweet, and our personal projections about the situation led us to opposite conclusions.

My friend believes the only reason Barr would use the *Planet of the Apes* reference with Jarrett is if she understood Jarrett was black. This implies that Barr, a Trump supporter, is actively racist.

Barr claimed the tweet was political in nature and had nothing to do with Jarrett's race, as she thought Jarrett was white. I believe her. Being racist is one of the biggest sins in America today, and racial issues are part of the daily news cycle. As a public figure, Barr understands this. I don't think she's racist, and it doesn't seem reasonable to me that she would risk her livelihood over a tweet.

My friend and I are reasonable men, but our personal sensibilities about this incident are opposite. We have different opinions about her intent that make sense to us, and we will brand her one way or the other based on them.

---

4   David Moye, "'Morning Joe' Host Says Trump Is 'Openly Racist' And So Are His Supporters," *Huffington Post,* June 22, 2018, https://www.huffingtonpost.com/entry/morning-joe-trump-openly-racist_us_5b2d1212e4b0321a01d0b1d5

5   Tom Elliott, "Media to Trump Voters: We Love You Racist, Nazi Scum!" *Townhall,* June 26, 2018, https://townhall.com/notebook/tomelliott/2018/06/26/media-to-trump-voters-we-love-you-racist-nazi-scum-n2494660

To half of America, she's a raging racist. To the other half, she isn't. It can't be both.

Stereotyping and imputing the intent of others can be dangerous, and it's contributing to the divide in our country today. The senses we rely on to help interpret the reality of this world often lead us astray. So what does any of this have to do with heightism, the victim mentality, or identity politics?

I want you to change your frequency and tune into something you may not be familiar or agree with.

Consider that the way we're dealing with discrimination in society is ineffective and counterproductive. Consider that identity politics and the symptoms associated with it, such as a victim mentality, are dividing our country instead of bringing us together. Consider that unjustly stereotyping and imputing intent to others is a narrow way of thinking and enhancing the tensions of society.

I may be wrong about all of this, but I'm becoming more comfortable with that.

Maybe making catchy signs, rallying in the streets, and shouting down people you disagree with is the way to go about changing society.

Maybe expecting others to change when we are unwilling to change ourselves is the way to stop discrimination.

Maybe having a victim mentality and blaming others for our shortcomings is the way to gain respect from our peers, and an even better way to lead a happy life.

Maybe segregating ourselves into our own echo chambers is the key to a diverse nation and living in harmony with each other.

Maybe. But I doubt it.

If what we're doing isn't working, and we're becoming increasingly divided, maybe it's time to switch things up a bit.

As you'll see, that's ultimately up to you.

Table of Contents

Introduction

My driver's license indicates I'm five feet six inches.[6]

It lies.

I'm a towering five foot five on a good day, but five foot eight in lifts. They're great if personal comfort isn't a priority.

I'm in the seventh percentile of height, meaning 93 percent of American men are taller than me.[7]

People have discriminated against me because of my height since the first grade. Whenever I voiced my concerns to anyone, they said it was all in my head, to ignore it, or "you're not *that* short."

God bless them all; they meant well.

My interest in studying heightism, or the discrimination against short people, began during my years at Boise State University (Go Broncos!) while earning my bachelor's degree in communication/journalism.

Reading academic papers on heightism validated my life experiences.

I became obsessed with it.

That's when I caught a bad case of victim mentality.

---

6   I have since rectified this lie.
7   "Height Percentile Calculator, by Age or Country," https://tall.life/height-percentile-calculator-age-country/

I saw heightism everywhere. I *wanted* to see it and was on the look-out for it. The more I saw it, the more it validated my feelings and experiences.

I saw heightism in places it didn't exist. For instance, I was too short to be Buster Bronco, the school mascot, because the costume was too big. I was outraged at the blatant discrimination. I wanted to be Buster but was automatically disqualified from trying out because I was too short. And nobody else seemed to care.

The victim mentality led to two decades of frustration, anger, and depression.

Living that life is like having a debit card with a million-dollar balance, but nobody gave you the PIN. Happiness is literally in your hands, but you can't access it because you don't know the code.

I believed I was a victim, and society was hell-bent on keeping me down. Life oftentimes felt hopeless.

My story isn't unique. Millions of people have the victim mentality whether they realize it or not.

Victim mentality is all the rage these days. It's a competition to win the biggest victim status, or as I call it, the Big Victim on Campus (BVOC). It's sad because I know its destructive nature firsthand.

It's embarrassing to admit I suffered from a victim mentality over something so goddamned silly.

Let's be honest; there's a good chance this is the first time you've heard about heightism, and there's an equally good chance you've already laughed about the concept.

That's okay. You're not alone.

Most people laugh, snicker, or look amused when they first hear about it.

... x ...

When introduced to the concept of heightism, many quickly dismiss it because they don't believe it exists, and, even if it does, it can't be too bad because they haven't heard about it before.

It's okay if that's you.[8]

Heightism is a discrimination based on something a person has no control over, just as with racism, sexism, and homophobia.

There are stereotypes associated with heightism. No doubt you've heard of the Napoleon complex[9] (NC) or think the only reason a short man works out or has a nice car is to compensate for being short.

While heightism is similar to other forms of discrimination, I'm the first to admit they are different beasts.

I'm not foolish enough to *equate* heightism to racism, sexism, and homophobia, but I am going to *compare* them. In doing so, I hope to highlight how society has embraced heightism in ways you aren't aware of.

To my knowledge, there are no formal groups plotting for the eradication of short people.

However, sperm banks refuse to let short men donate, and geneticists can identify embryos that will end up being shorter than normal. People don't want short children because, while they may not be consciously aware or educated on the concept of heightism, they understand the value of tallness.

Heightism is one of the last forms of socially accepted discrimination today, and people are reluctant to view short people, especially short men, as a marginalized group.

---

8   You should probably ditch that attitude though, you heightist!
9   The Napoleon complex is a misnomer, as Napoleon Bonaparte was five feet seven inches, which was the average height of Frenchmen at the time. Robert Wilde, "Was Napoleon Bonaparte Really Short? Napoleon's Height Revealed," *ThoughtCo,* Updated January 21, 2019, https://www.thoughtco.com/was-napoleon-bonaparte-short-1221108.

In one of the saddest segments in cable news history, the CNN show *Paula Zahn Now* took ninety-six precious seconds of airtime in 2007 to discuss proposed legislation in Massachusetts that would have given short people protection under the same laws as blacks and women (the legislation subsequently failed).[10]

The four-person panel, whose heights averaged six feet, concluded that, in this lawsuit-happy country, legislation wasn't the right way to go when dealing with height discrimination.[11] Ironically, three of the four panelists (two women and one black man) benefit from the protection of discrimination laws that they don't think short people should have access to.

As the panel members supposedly faced discrimination their entire lives for having vaginas or more melanin in their skin, you would assume they wouldn't want others to face similar discrimination. You'd also assume that they would be in favor of protecting short people under the same laws they benefit from. Right?

Right?

Apparently not.

It appears they don't want us in their exclusive victim club.

They lose nothing by allowing short people the same protections, except a special victim status that allows them to remain the BVOC.

It's a badge of honor to claim the discrimination they've faced is worse than what someone else has endured. That's the entire point of intersectionality.[12] It's a slick tactic to keep the focus on them at the exclusion of someone else. It's used to dismiss the real hardships of others.

---

10   "Paula Zahn Now – Heightism and Emails from Viewers," filmed March 19, 2007, video, 4:54, https://www.youtube.com/watch?v=jcJiU2dD53Q
11   Not surprisingly, they didn't offer any solutions either.
12   Factual Feminist, "Intersectional Feminism: What is it?" published March 30, 2016, video, 8:12, https://www.youtube.com/watch?v=cYpELqKZ02Q

Why else would vacuous organizations, such as Buzzfeed, among others, feel the need to have a "privilege test" that tells you how much of a victim you are based on your race, sex, or sexual orientation?[13] It's literally a hierarchy of oppression, assigning a number to your level of perceived victimhood, which is why many critics of identity politics call it the "oppression Olympics."

This is part of what's wrong with society today. People want the political[14] or social benefits of being the bigger victim, which is discrimination one-upmanship.

It's like the popular kids in high school who don't want the chess clubbers at their senior kegger. They all want to celebrate the end of their high school careers and the beginning of a new phase of life, but there's always someone trying to exclude those they don't see as worthy.

Those kids are assholes. Don't be those kids.

If you're against the discrimination you think you're facing, you should also be against the discrimination someone else is facing. Yet many in the protected groups play the exclusionary game and don't *really* want equality as they claim. They strive for special political and social consideration at the expense of others.

That makes them assholes.

If everybody who claims discrimination at the hands of others stopped discriminating against others, there wouldn't be much discrimination in America today.

---

13   Rega Jha and Tommy Wesely, "How Privileged Are You: Check(list) your privilege," *Buzzfeed,* April 10, 2014, https://www.buzzfeed.com/regajha/how-privileged-are-you?utm_term=. ImaekzxN8#.rnVpn18qv

14   Bruce Thornton, "The Politics of Victimhood," *Hoover Institution,* October 16, 2014, https:// www.hoover.org/research/politics-victimhood

Main Objectives

First, this book is meant to highlight the ugliness of heightism. I hope you leave understanding it's a real thing that shouldn't exist, just like other forms of unjust discrimination.

Second, it's about calling out those who voluntarily make themselves a victim when they weren't a victim of discrimination in the first place. For example, people with a victim mentality do this when they accuse others of committing microaggressions against them. Sometimes people flat-out lie about circumstances and events to get attention as a victim, such as with NFL player Michael Bennett (see chapter 2). The lies stoke the flames of social outrage, thus enhancing the status of the "victim" while wrongly painting a negative picture of the individuals or institutions that have been accused of the wrongdoing.

Third, this is written from a male perspective. My focus is discrimination against short men. It's not meant to exclude short women. Heightism tends to hit men in unique ways that it doesn't women.

Fourth, challenge yourself to see things from a different perspective, to change your frequency, and to listen with an open mind. See how ignorant it is for people to accept heightism but shun other forms of discrimination with the righteous indignation they deserve. Realize how society's acceptance of heightism is absurd and horrific when compared to racism, sexism, and homophobia.

Fifth, this book may assist people in other marginalized groups with similar struggles like me. Unlike other movements, my objective is to help end discrimination for all, not just those in my demographic, and there may be information here to aid in achieving that goal.

Sixth, we must work on overhauling ourselves rather than expecting others to change to appease us. Isn't it great to train dogs to do what we demand of them? We can't expect other humans to bow to our every desire like canines do.

Lastly, I wish to destroy Buzzfeed.[15]

If you're the type of person who needs a trigger warning, consider this your warning.

My opinions may anger and offend you. You may disagree with me, and that's okay. The important thing is to listen and keep an open mind.

Despite our potential differences in philosophies, I have only the best of intentions for everybody.[16] Let's start with two premises I think we can all agree on: unjust discrimination shouldn't exist, and we all have the best of intentions for society.

Because I want you to listen and keep an open mind, it would be hypocritical of me not to do the same thing. If you think you can change my mind or just want to further discuss any topic, feel free to contact me at the email below. I'll only reply to serious and respectful inquiries.

This is my attempt to make this world of ours a better place to live.

Act accordingly.

Leslie Bingham

Lesliebinghamwrites@gmail.com

---

15 Just before publication of this book, Buzzfeed announced it was going to lay off 15 percent of its staff. I'm pretty sure they did it in anticipation of this book, but I have not confirmed that yet.
16 Except Buzzfeed. #Buzzfeedcaneatshitanddie

CHAPTER 1:

The Realization

Starting defense! Place at the table! Wooooooooooo!
— Steve Lattimer in *The Program*

My senior year swagger was sickening. I reeked of confidence. Maybe it was the Drakkar Noir. Regardless, the 1996–97 school year was my year. Nay, it was *our* year! We were like no other class in the history of high schools. Our badassery was epic.

Yeah, you know the feeling.

After an early-morning football practice, Coach Weiser named me one of the full-season captains. I drove home in my cream-colored 1980 Cutlass Supreme and yelled, "Fuck yes!" at the top of my lungs.

Think of the 1993 hit movie *The Program* when Lattimer makes start-ing defense. That was me, sans head-smashing car windows and inject-ing steroids.

As the smallest guy on the Ronan Chiefs squad, towering at five foot four, I felt at least five foot ten in that moment. I mean, I imagine taller people always feel like champions. The years of sweat, broken bones, ill-advised mullets, and dreams of greatness were coming together for the perfect end of an era.

Team Captains Matt Kocubinski, Skip Bingham, Frank Webster, and Nick Clary await the coin toss.

This was the stuff of inspirational movies — *Rudy, Rocky, Secretariat, Hoosiers*. We were destined to be the next one-word megahit sports movie: *Chiefs*.

We were bringing gridiron glory back to the little reservation school. Anything short of a deep playoff run was incomprehensible.

We finished 1–6, but I digress.

Nabbing your preferred number was always a big deal. Joe Peabody was number eleven because, as he liked to say, "I'm twice as good as everyone else." Matt Kocubinski got number sixty-nine because duh.

My dad died on February 16, 1988, in a car accident. I was nine years old. To honor him, I simply added two (representing the second month) to the one in sixteen and came up with thirty-six. It was a bit silly and cryptic, and nobody knew but me (and of course my dad, who was no doubt smiling from above), but it was important.

The day we chose our numbers was the day the assistant coach took our height and weight for the team roster.

"All right, Mr. Bingham, what ya got?"

"Number thirty-six, five feet four inches, one hundred twenty-five pounds!"

He wrote it down and then paused. The pencil hovered above the paper for a couple of seconds as if contemplating life itself. He then scribbled down five foot six, one hundred thirty-five.[17]

"Looks like you grew a little this year," he said.

Despite adding two inches and ten pounds with the simple stroke of a scuffed #2 pencil with chew marks, it felt like he chop-blocked me at the knees. My head, once above the clouds, was stuck in a fog.

---

[17] I found out twenty years later, thanks to number sixty-nine, the coaches increased the height and weight of most players on the team. Intimidation, man, it's part of the game.

I'm not naive. We all strive to be bigger and stronger than our opponent. It's an obvious competitive advantage. That's what all the gym hours were for.

Trust me, I was aware of how much bigger my teammates were. A day without them making fun of my shortness was as rare as the day science discovered a rainbow-shitting albino unicorn.

But this was different.

This was an adult telling me bigger is better. Bigger is respect. You, Mr. Bingham, at your current height and weight, aren't worthy of the Chiefs' roster.

I'd never considered lying about my height before. I certainly didn't think the coaches would feel the need to lie about it, considering I was a wide receiver.

Especially considering that Shalon Baker, the five-foot-seven (on a good day) wide receiver and 1994 graduate of the University of Montana, tore up college defenses week after week, and he was playing professionally in Canada at the time. I lived sixty miles north of Missoula, all the sports fans in town knew about him. Sure, he was quick and skilled — two things I lacked — but we admired his success, especially because of his size.

I understand increasing the personal information of linebackers, linemen, or running backs. But *receiver*? I wasn't hitting anyone. I was trying to run crisp routes to get open to catch a ball. I was a backup anyway, to Joe Peabody, because he was twice as good as me.

Bigger and stronger was more desirable at every position. Even with the little lie going down on the official team roster, I was still the smallest guy on the team. By far.

Despite my huge ego and supreme confidence at the time, I felt insignificant in that moment.

That moment was so poignant because my coaches were more important to me than they were for the average kid.

After my dad passed, part of my coping mechanism included immersing myself in academics and sports. I craved to make him proud every day, and I thought making my teachers and coaches pleased with my performance was the way to accomplish that.

They were my father figures. I watched how they operated, interacted with each other, and disciplined because they were my gauge on how to become a man.

They taught me integrity.

Case in point: At the end of a practice the year prior, Coach Weiser told us they accidentally allowed an ineligible player to play. He had two options: keep the rule violation a secret, as nobody would have ever found out, or report the violation to the Montana High School Association because the integrity of the football program was more important.

He chose option two, and we forfeited several early-season wins that eliminated us from postseason consideration as a result.

We all felt like Tom Brady's deflated footballs.

Of course, my coaches, and sports in general, taught me the importance of personal responsibility and the value of competition.

Be accountable to yourself. Be accountable to your teammates. Be better than the person lining up across from you.

Your success is dependent on your personal accountability.

My coaches also unwittingly taught me about lack of respect for shorter men.

A silly football roster showed me that even adults put a premium on being bigger, taller, and stronger. It's more respectable than shorter and smaller.

While I worked my way to popularity and was well liked,[18] it wasn't easy growing up (ha!) as one of the smallest boys, no matter what room I strutted into. I dreamed of a future when people would respect me as an equal. No more jokes, disrespect, or people looking at me like I was less than them.

That adult utopia doesn't exist.

Yet.

———————— ◆ ————————

The first time I felt different because of my height was picture day in elementary school.

It was a beautiful late-summer day in 1986. The ever-kind Mrs. Ostermayer, my first grade teacher, instructed us to line up from shortest to tallest.

I was the shortest boy in class, and despite the clear instructions, I wanted to stand next to the taller boys to avoid being next to the girls because girls were gross. I didn't want to parade my new red shirt and homemade haircut next to them.

One of the taller boys in class, a complete jerk face, smugly said, "You have to go to the front of the line!"

My eyes widened, and my heart paced. Not only did Smugly McJerkface call me out publicly, but he also got great pleasure out of it.

There was one girl in class shorter than me, but it was close. We stood back to back; the entire time I tried to avoid touching her because …

---

18   That's how I choose to remember it, anyway.

gross. I stretched my spine as far as it would go and avoided getting on my tippy-toes because that's cheating, and cheating is bad.

After the madness and confusion of perfectly lining up by height, the shortest boys were forced to kneel on the floor because a girl's dress is too precious to mess. The shortest girls sat right behind us. And the taller kids, Smugly McJerkface among them, got the privilege of standing in the back two rows, lording their tallness over the rest of us.

I was displeased. Wouldn't it make more sense for the tall kids to sit on the floor? They're already so tall, why do they have to look taller? And why did I have to kneel on the grimy floor — no doubt loaded with recess scum, feces, boogers, and other people's hair and spittle — and get my new blue jeans dirty when others got to sit on benches or stand comfortably?

It's not a malicious practice for schools to line up kids from shortest to tallest for class pictures, but it sends a message at an early age that height is a desired attribute.

Our everyday lives are littered with language that reinforces this idea. Mom always encouraged me to eat my disgusting vegetables and drink my milk so I could become big and strong like my oldest brother, Tony, who is six feet. There are phrases and words such as "Don't look/ talk down to others" and "Stand tall" and "shortcomings." You get the point.

I was anxious during doctor visits when they checked my height progress versus the national averages. "Don't worry," I recall a doctor telling me in middle school, "many boys have growth spurts later in life. I know a guy who grew four inches between the ages of eighteen and twenty!"

Doctors can be vicious liars.

"Powerful things come in small packages" was one of my mom's favorite sayings. Like diamond rings, you know? A girl's best friend!

But I didn't want to be a diamond ring. I wanted to be tall. And women prefer the bigger diamonds anyway.

Journalist John Stossel described an experiment with elementary school students and their preference for taller men:

> ABCNews gave elementary school students a test, asking them to match a small, medium or large figure of a man with a series of words. The kids overwhelmingly linked the tall figure to the words strong, handsome, and smart. They linked the short figure to the words sad, scared and weak. More than half the kids also chose to link the short figure to the words dumb, yucky, and no friends.[19]

Kids are naturally drawn to their taller peers and at the same time repelled by the shorter ones.

---

19   John Stossel, "The Ugly Truth About Beauty," *ABC News,* https://abcnews.go.com/2020/ story?id=123853&page=1

I was no different. I felt the gravitational pull of the taller kids and wanted to be included in their activities. Recess was supposed to be a time to have fun and make friends, but I was rejected time and again by the taller kids playing basketball. I spent my recesses alone at the netless basketball hoop practicing my long-range jumper with a dodgeball because they had all the real basketballs.

At the netless hoop, imagined swishes could have been air balls.

After numerous rejections, I quit trying to be their friend or to play with them and learned my place on the playground was the shitty hoop. I was sad and had the stereotypical redhead/short-boy temper. Other kids don't like that kid.

I thought taking first place in the three-legged race and third place in the wheelbarrow race during a track-and-field day would help change their minds about me, but I got no cool points or friends from my accomplishments because I was matched up with a girl for both competitions. You must be close to the same height as your partner for those races, and the only person left that met the criteria was a girl. And I had to touch her.

Gross.

On the plus side, there was no danger of popularity, so I focused on doing math really, really fast. I was the fastest adder and subtracter in the class.

That's cool in elementary school, right?[20]

We moved from Idaho to Montana the summer after first grade. Others bullied me for being the new, short, redheaded kid on the Flathead Indian Reservation.

I waded chest deep in the sewers of growing up short and as a minority in my own neighborhood. My mom is an enrolled member of the

---

20   Nope.

Confederated Salish and Kootenai Tribes of the Flathead Indian nation, so even though we have white freckled skin, we lived in an Indian housing development among other poor, mainly Native American families.

I didn't understand when classmates yelled at me in the hallways at school for stealing their land. I didn't understand when our neighborhood friends stopped coming over to our house to play football, or why some threw rocks at me while waiting for the school bus.

People discriminated against me for being short and for the color of my skin.

As the years wore on, I learned how to deal with it all. I learned to make fun of myself before others could and to laugh at their jokes if they got to the punchline first. I learned to hide my anger. Others eventually accepted me, which turned into real friendships and a fulfilling high school career. I was still a punching bag and the butt of jokes, but it was a small price to pay for friendships.

Society has become more conscientious about bullying. The federal government has an entire website dedicated to the matter.[21] It lists kids who are most at risk of being bullied. It includes the LGBT community; youth with disabilities or other special health needs; kids of different races, ethnicities, and national origin; and those with different religions or faiths. Overweight and underweight youth get a special shout-out as well.

The closest the site gets to mentioning short people is when it says those who "are perceived as weak or unable to defend themselves." That can include anyone.

The website focuses on the groups the federal government already protects with antidiscrimination laws. It's illegal to discriminate against others based on race, color, religion, sex, sexual orientation,

---

21   Stopbullying.gov

and national origin.[22] If you bully or make fun of someone who belongs in these groups, you're labeled a racist, a sexist, a homophobe, or a xenophobe.

You would never know by reading the website that short people (especially short boys) are mentally and physically bullied and discriminated against.

If you don't belong to one of the popular victim groups, nobody seems to care about the discrimination you face.

The federal government perpetuates the notion that to be a proper victim, you must be part of the protected classes. If you don't fall into one of these groups, pull up your big-boy pants, Jack; it can't be that bad!

Short boys are not worth mentioning on the federal government's antibullying website. Short people are not seen as worthy of federal protections against discrimination.

It's little wonder that heightism is one of the few accepted forms of discrimination today.

---

22   "Prohibited Employment Policies/Practices," U.S. Equal Employment Opportunity Commission, https://www.eeoc.gov/laws/practices/index.cfm

CHAPTER 2:

Playing the Victim

The minute you think of yourself as a victim, you've
given control of your life to someone else.
— Condoleezza Rice

I am not a product of my circumstances.
I am a product of my choices.
— Tom Bilyeu

You're only a victim for as long as you want to be.
— Leslie Bingham

Kathy Griffin posted a photograph of herself online gripping a fake, severed head of President Donald Trump. Most people on both sides of the political spectrum found the photo atrocious. The Trump family took to Twitter and voiced their disgust. Because of her choices, she lost her New Year's Eve gig at CNN, and several of her stand-up acts got canceled.

Griffin and her lawyer set up an embarrassing press conference where Griffin played the victim. She stated, "What's happening to me has never happened, ever, in the history of this great country. A sitting president of the United States, and his grown children, and the First Lady, are personally, I feel, trying to ruin my life forever. This bully, this president, of all people, is gonna come after me? He picked the wrong redhead ... I'm gonna be honest ... he broke me. He broke me. He broke me."[23]

In 2015, on the campus of Vanderbilt University, someone left a bag of feces on the porch of the university's Black Cultural Center. It occurred a day after black students protested perceived racism on campus. They rushed to Facebook to denounce the deplorable hate crime and vowed, "We will not allow for the desecration of the place we call home."

A blind woman who couldn't find a trash can left the dog poop on the porch. She did her duty, which was to leave it by the closest doorstep she could find for someone to throw away.[24]

Evergreen State College students lost their minds after Professor Bret Weinstein disagreed with the tactics of the people promoting the school's annual Day of Absence. Previously, minority students left campus to participate in programs and discussions about race issues, but they wanted white students to stay off campus for the day.

Weinstein, who favors the Day of Absence, thought making white students stay off campus was a bad idea. As he has white skin and disagreed with the group's tactics, they branded him a racist. Students protested and demanded their fellow progressive to either resign or be fired. By doing so, the students pulled out their victim cards, railing against everything white with chants of "Hey-hey, ho-ho, these racist teachers have got to go," and a student proclaimed to raucous

---

23   "Kathy Griffin on Donald Trump phot scandal," streamed live on June 2, 2017, video, 22:10, https://www.youtube.com/watch?v=_wKV-D895t4

24   Jeff Woods, "Bag of Dog Poop Causes Big Stir on Vandy Campus," *Nashville Scene,* November 19, 2015, https://www.nashvillescene.com/news/pith-in-the-wind/article/13062140/bag-of-dog-poop-causes-big-stir-on-vandy-campus

applause, "Whiteness is the most fucking violent system to ever breathe."[25]

Someone graffitied a racial slur on the gate to Lebron James's mansion in Los Angeles the night before his Cleveland Cavaliers took on the Golden State Warriors for game one of the 2017 NBA finals. When asked about it at a press conference, James likened the graffiti to the brutal murder of Emmett Till, a black boy in Mississippi who was lynched in 1955 for whistling at a white woman.[26]

It remains unclear how graffiti correlates to an unjust murder. It also remains a mystery who committed this hate crime.[27] But James dug deep to equate his victimhood to that of a true victim in Till.

This is a mere smattering of people clamoring to make themselves the BVOC.

Isn't it astonishing that these victims have somehow gained psychic abilities and can determine the intent of their alleged victimizers?

Griffin *feels* the Trumps' intentions are to destroy her. The students at Vanderbilt *felt* the bag of dog poo was a bigoted act. The students at Evergreen *knew* their professor was racist because he dared to criticize their bully tactics. And James *knows* the graffiti is proof of racism despite knowing nothing about the spray painter.

These victims jump to conclusions based on their feelings, not necessarily on the reality of the situation. They make a mockery of real victims, and their claims detract from real bullying and discrimination.

---

25 "Students takeover of Evergreen State College," published on May 27, 2017, video, 7:14, https://www.youtube.com/watch?v=bO1agIILlhg

26 "C'mon, LeBron, Your Emmett Till Analogy Is Simply Cavalier," *Wall Street Journal Opinion,* June 4, 2017, https://www.wsj.com/articles/cmon-lebron-your-emmett-till-analogy-is-simply-cavalier-1496605156

27 Serious question: is it still considered a hate crime if another black person committed the act? As of the writing of this book, there are still no suspects.

By choosing to play the victim, they give up their personal power to outside forces, their supposed victimizers, who may not harbor the intent to which they are ascribing.

The tweet that destroyed and broke Griffin? "Kathy Griffin should be ashamed of herself. My children, especially my 11 year old son, Barron, are having a hard time with this. Sick!" This isn't a destructive or breaking tweet unless you've taken the victim road most traveled and choose to let it be destructive.

The Vanderbilt students had nothing to be upset about, but they chose to be based on what they *felt* was a nefarious act.

The children of Evergreen fought against no racism with fanfare, anger, and vitriol. They *felt* their professor was racist and ironically became the bullies they claimed to fight against. Their mob mentality and bully tactics prompted Weinstein to sue the school. He was subsequently awarded $500,000 and resigned from his faculty position.

Despite Lebron James somehow linking Graffitigate to a racially based murder, there's only conjecture of racist intent, as there's still no evidence in the case.

Ascribing racist, sexist, or heightist intent with no proof except your feelings gives power to a faceless entity of what I call "ethereal discrimination" that's floating around the sky. It suppresses people based on the amount of melanin in their skin, the genitals they possess, or their height relative to the norm. It's scanning the horizons for marginalized groups so it can, well, suppress them, I suppose.

Ethereal discrimination lives only in the heads of the people who have chosen to adopt a victim mentality.

It's sad that I must clarify this, but unfortunately the political climate of today demands it. Let's be clear: There are real victims who deserve our support. People have suffered greatly because someone else didn't like the color of their skin, their genitalia, their height, their religion, or who they sleep with in the privacy of their own home. It's unacceptable that these types of victims exist.

But let's also be clear: My examples do not encompass real victims. My examples include people who have made themselves victims in their own minds. In today's culture, this sort of victimhood is skyrocketing.

The Merriam-Webster dictionary definition of *victim mentality* is simply "the belief that one is always a victim: the idea that bad things will always happen to one."

Fleshed out, the victim mentality "is a psychological term that refers to a type of dysfunctional mindset which seeks to feel persecuted in order to gain attention or avoid self-responsibility. People who struggle with the victim mentality are convinced that life is not only beyond their control, but is out to deliberately hurt them. This belief results in constant blame, finger-pointing, and pity parties that are fueled by pessimism, fear, and anger."[28]

We all know what this looks like with the people we encounter in our lives. It's also a sight to see when the rich and powerful fall to this mentality. Let's look at an example from the 2018 US Open tennis tournament involving Serena Williams, one of the most accomplished tennis players of all time.

The facts are simple. Williams received a code violation warning because her coach was coaching from the stands, which is against the rules. The second code violation was for smashing her racket. Two violations equal a point penalty. This is when her victim mentality began to shine. She complained to chair umpire Carlos Ramos, who imposed the penalties, "Every time I play here, I have problems. I did not

---

28   Mateo Sol, "23 Signs You're Suffering From a Victim Mentality," https://lonerwolf.com/victim-mentality/

have coaching. I don't cheat. You need to make an announcement. I have a daughter, and I stand for what's right. You owe me an apology."

Shortly thereafter, she verbally abused Ramos, resulting in her third code violation and a game penalty. Williams continued her strong victim game by appealing to referee Brian Earley, saying, in part, "There's a lot of men out here who have said a lot of things. It's because I am a woman, and that's not right ... This always happens to me!"

She persisted with the sexism theme after the match: "I can't sit here and say I wouldn't say he's a thief because I thought he took a game from me, but I've seen other men call other umpires several things, and I'm here fighting for women's rights and for women's equality and for all kinds of stuff. And for me to say 'thief,' and for him to take the game, it made me feel like it was a sexist remark. He's never took a game from a man because they said 'thief.'"

Unfortunately, for Williams, the numbers don't back up her claims of sexism. Men were handed out eighty-six code violations at the 2018 US Open, but women only received twenty-two. Additionally, over the past twenty years at grand-slam events, men have been given 1,534 code violations and women only 526.[29]

As a sports fan and former athlete, I understand the frustration when calls don't go your way and officials seemingly lack consistency. I also understand 100 percent consistency isn't always possible as either an official or a player.

Ramos issued Novak Djokovic a warning for throwing his racket at Wimbledon in 2018, whereas in the same match, his opponent did the same thing and was not penalized. Djokovic accused Ramos of having "double standards."[30]

29 Simon Briggs, "Carlos Ramos returns to umpire's chair after Serena Williams row as statistics back him up," The Telegraph, September 14, 2018, https://www.telegraph.co.uk/tennis/2018/09/13/carlos-ramos-returns-chair-serena-williams-row-statistics-back/

30 Tom Lutz, "It's not just Serena: how umpire Carlos Ramos has clashed with players," The Guardian, September 9, 2018, https://www.theguardian.com/sport/2018/sep/09/carlos-ramos-serena-williams-tennis-umpire-us-open

We can all blame Ramos, who has been criticized for years as being a stickler for the rules, for making bad calls. I think the calls against Williams were terrible, and I get why she was angry. But to slander the man with claims of sexism is unwarranted.

Do you think she would have called a female umpire making the same calls a sexist? Of course not.

At the 2011 US Open, chair umpire Eva Asderaki gave Williams a penalty, and she flew into a verbal tirade that included, "Aren't you the one that screwed me over last time here? Yeah, you are. Seriously, you have it out for me? ... You're a hater, and you're just unattractive inside ... What a loser."[31]

The pattern is simple. When something doesn't go her way, it's because of sexism or someone else screwing her over because for some unknown reason they want her to fail. When she cries, "This always happens to me," she's not taking personal responsibility for the actions that got her into these situations. It's always something happening to her, something out of her control.

It's the antithesis of what we're all supposed to learn from sports, which is why I unfortunately lost most of my respect for Williams after her latest diatribe.

Did anyone else notice the hypocrisy in Williams calling Ramos a sexist? Because she wouldn't call another woman sexist, it appears as if Williams may be the only sexist in this scenario.

Lobbing complaints against certain groups of people is prejudiced. Williams obviously felt justified accusing a man of sexism. She even complained that she'd seen male players get away with much worse, implying that other male umpires are more tolerant of men and allow

---

31   Alanah Eriksen, "'I truly despise you and you're unattractive inside,': Serena Williams' extraordinary outburst at U.S. Open umpire lands her a $2,000 fine," *Daily Mail,* September 12, 2011, https://www.dailymail.co.uk/news/article-2036471/Serena-Williams-US-Open-outburst-2011-final-umpire-I-truly-despise-you.html

them to get away with throwing temper tantrums that she can't get away with. That, my friends, is a sexist attitude toward men.

Imagine a woman umpire giving five-foot-nine ex-professional tennis player Michael Chang a penalty and him calling her out for being sexist. How many people would agree with him, given that men are penalized three times as much as women?[32]

Now imagine after she gave him a penalty, he called her out for being a heightist, and that she would never give a taller player the same penalty. How many people would agree with him (if they could even get their thoughts out through fits of hysterical laughter)?[33]

These examples are as ludicrous and valid as Williams's claim of sexism. The only difference is that some outlandish claims are accepted by societal orthodoxy and others aren't.

Most so-called microaggressions fall under the umbrella of ethereal discrimination.

Microaggressions.com is a blog called the Microagression Project, started by two Columbia University students. They encourage people to submit their experiences with microaggressions for publication on the site. Below are a few of the submissions I came across while perusing the page:

> The offending statement: "Look, it's a dog walker, you have such a cool job!" (said) A white woman in the lobby of my condo. To which I replied, "These are my dogs and I live here." Her [totally oblivious] "Oh! He does too!" I shook my head and got into the elevator. It felt as if she were implying that a (sic) Afro-American person – much less a woman — could (sic) afford to

---

32   Zero. Zero people would agree with him.
33   Zero. Zero people would take this claim seriously. He would forever be known as the world's most pathetic crybaby man.

live in this building.

The offending statement: "I mean it's morally wrong to fire people because they're gay, but that doesn't mean that it should be illegal!" My brother, a straight white man who has never had to fear discrimination in the workplace.

The offending statement: "I don't like short hair on girls." Random older men to me, a woman, when I got an undercut for the first time. In a tone of voice that suggests they think their word is law.

The submission: Sometimes when I say I'm from Detroit, people's tone of voice becomes uneasy. They might even cringe. One even said that they never guessed, as though where one lives should be obvious. It's a shame that people think I'm a criminal just because of where I live.

The offending statement: "Can you provide specific examples of the sexism and transphobia you have experienced, so the board can decide if training is necessary." Response from the Board of Directors to my request for anti-sexism and anti-transphobia for a queer organization I belong to.

The offending statement: "Meet any nice boys?" My mother, aunt, and grandmother whenever I come home from college.[34]

The "dog walker" woman based the perceived racist statement on her *feelings*, not necessarily the facts of the situation. As in the Serena Williams example earlier, the black woman who wrote this submission may be the only individual in this situation being prejudiced and making racist assumptions. She thought the white woman was assuming she couldn't afford to live there. Her assumption was based on the

---

34   All six statements/scenarios are from different people and posted to the blog http://www.microaggressions.com/.

color of the other person's skin, which is racist. She would not believe this would be a microaggression if the offender were black instead of white.

The straight white brother who doesn't think it should be illegal to fire someone based on their sexuality, though he admits doing so is morally wrong, has a difference of opinion about the law. It's not a homophobic statement.

Dear short-haired lady, I don't care for undercuts on women either, just like the older men you complain about. It's a personal preference, just as some women don't like long hair or shaved heads on men. Would you consider it a microaggression when women used to tell me they didn't like mullets on men?

Dear Detroit: How in the world do you know these people think you're a criminal? I'd cringe because it seems like a shitty place to live.

A board of directors asking follow-up questions to a request isn't a microaggression or transphobic; it's them doing their due diligence as a board of directors.

When I was in college, my mom always asked me, "Meet any nice girls?" It's a normal question for parents to ask their children. Isn't meeting people supposed to be part of the college experience?

Were you offended by any of the microaggressions above?

A microaggression is subjective to the individual who *feels* someone else made a prejudicial statement or act toward them. A microaggression to one person isn't a microaggression to someone who doesn't choose to be a victim.

If the dog-walker situation happened to two black women, and one found the statement offensive but the other didn't, who gets to act as the authority in determining if it's a microaggression? How can it be a microaggression to one but not the other? Who decides if the words uttered are based in racism?

Choosing to play the victim is the problem of the individual who feels aggressed upon, not the alleged offender.

In an article written for *Scientific American*, Scott Lilienfeld, a professor of psychology at Emory University, writes:

> For one thing, microaggressions as [psychologist Derald Wing] Sue and others conceptualize them lie entirely in the eyes of the beholder. Therefore, if a person feels "microaggressed" against, he or she is automatically deemed to be the victim of a microaggression. The problems here are twofold: First, if person A is offended by the statement but person B is not, this would mean it both is and is not a microaggression, a proposition that is patently illogical. Second, science hinges on the ability to corroborate findings using converging sources of evidence. If a concept is entirely subjective, it is exceedingly difficult to study it scientifically, let alone subject it to rigorous tests ... Psychological research demonstrates that if person A believes that person B's actions are intentionally hostile, he or she is more likely to respond aggressively in turn. People's perceived motives matter.

> The science aside, it is crucial to ask whether conceptualizing the interpersonal world in terms of microaggressions does more good than harm. The answer is "We don't know." Still, there are reasons for concern. Encouraging individuals to be on the lookout for subtle, in some cases barely discernible, signs of prejudice in others puts just about everyone on the defensive. Minority individuals are likely to become chronically

vigilant to minor indications of potential psychological harm whereas majority individuals are likely to feel a need to walk on eggshells, closely monitoring their every word and action to avoid offending others. As a consequence, microaggression training may merely ramp up already simmering racial tensions.[35]

The article also states, "When encountered frequently over long stretches of time, Sue and colleagues argue, microaggressions exert a detrimental impact on recipients, contributing to low self-esteem and, in some cases, clinical levels of depression, anxiety, and other mental health problems."

Choosing to play the victim and giving up your personal power to ethereal discrimination, such as perceived microaggressions, is like losing an arm-wrestling match to a mannequin.

I lost that match many times.

I chose to play the victim for over a decade. I had a bad case of the victim mentality (henceforth known as VM) because I was unhappy about my height and thought others perceived me as inferior because of it.

Just as in the earlier examples, I ascribed intent to others. I thought I knew their intentions better than they did. In believing this, I was on a mission to be the victim.

By believing others made microaggressions against me, I became angry and depressed and had negative views of not only society at large but also of myself.

I know how psychologically dangerous it is to give up my personal power to a stranger whom I thought mistreated me by uttering

---

35 Scott Lilienfeld, "The Science of Microaggressions: It's Complicated," *Scientific American,* June 23, 2017, https://blogs.scientificamerican.com/observations/the-science-of-microaggressions-its-complicated/

something I believed was heightist or by looking at me in a way I believed was condescending.

I was like Serena Williams and the black lady who felt wronged when someone thought she was a dog walker. I assumed others held a negative bias against me, and that resulted in me having a negative bias against them.

I couldn't comprehend my own hypocrisy or that I engaged in the same behavior as those I thought were wronging me.

Besides, even if people do have a negative bias against me, so what? I made the mistake of making that my problem when it shouldn't have affected my life at all.

I lived with the VM for a long time, so it's easy for me to spot it in others. It's becoming a much larger problem in society than most people think. My criticism of others (which is the same as my criticism of myself) isn't to shame them; it's to help illustrate how people are making themselves the BVOC so you can avoid falling into the VM trap like I did. Nobody should go through life feeling like a victim. That doesn't make for a healthy society, and it certainly doesn't make for a healthy you.

———— • ————

Game Time!

What's Happening in This Scene?

A bald, white man sits alone at the bar of a downtown Portland, Oregon, establishment. He is wearing a tight black T-shirt with a coiled snake on the front.

A black man with a bushy beard and a white woman arrive and sit three stools away. The bald man intermittently looks at the couple in a rather intense, serious, and concentrated manner. He then finishes his beer and pays his tab.

Before leaving, he looks at the couple one last time. The couple stares him down menacingly. The bald man quickly gets up from his barstool and exits the establishment.

Does He or Doesn't He Take Offense?

A six-foot cashier at the movie theater concession counter asks the five-foot-five man he's serving, "Hey, big guy, what'll it be?"

He Considered *That* a Microaggression?

A short, confident man works as a waiter at a restaurant next to the local university. Four attractive college women sit in his section. He saunters to the table, nails the service like nobody's business, and as he walks away to place the order with the cooks, all four women giggle and then burst into laughter.

Pop Quiz

What do you do if you see a banana peel in a tree?

Lies Hurt Real Victims

What do Michael Bennett, Dauntarius Williams, Yasmin Seweid, Pastor Jordan Brown, and an anonymous black cadet at the Air Force Academy have in common?

(See the end of the chapter for answers.)

————— ◆ —————

Learning about heightism in college was validating. On one hand, I had academic proof that heightism was real. On the other hand, I found a sick satisfaction in playing the victim. I saw heightism where it didn't exist in the form of microaggressions because I *wanted* to see it everywhere.

I felt both intellectually and morally superior to the people who I thought discriminated against me. I felt intellectually superior because I had knowledge of something they knew nothing about; nobody I knew had ever heard about heightism before. I felt morally superior because I *knew* my discriminators were probably against other forms of discrimination based on physical characteristics. To me, it was a sign of straight-up hypocrisy, moral bankruptcy, or ignorance.

I was, of course, quick to judge others because I thought I was more virtuous than they, not comprehending I was judging them the same way I thought they were judging me.

While I felt superior, I gave my discriminators powers they didn't know they possessed.

I could have hand-delivered a beautifully wrapped package, complete with a red bow, to each of them. The calligraphed note inside would say, "My personal power belongs to you now." These complete strangers would look at me and think, "What the fuck is wrong with this guy? What did I do to deserve this exquisitely wrapped gift? What do I do with a stranger's personal power? Is it rude to reject, regift, or sell it for cash? Is it cheap of me to keep the bow for future use?"

It's a ridiculous concept to think about literally, but I metaphorically did this all the time. People with a VM do this daily.

There were times I was more worried about a stranger's perception of me than I was on living my own life.

Complaining about any of this was out of the question, though, as I was in a no-win situation.

To begin with, I have a penis, and people with penises aren't supposed to complain lest they be tagged a whiny little bitch. So sayeth society.

I have a penis and I'm short, so I'm doubly screwed. If I complain, people accuse me of having the Napoleon complex, thus perpetuating the stereotype of angry little men everywhere. So sayeth society yet again.

I could have complained and have people think I was a wuss with little man's syndrome and perpetuate the stereotype, or I could have remained silent to stew in my own little broth of self-loathing salts and sadness herbs.

So I stewed and damaged my mental health.

And wouldn't you know, the ethereal heightism, as opposed to the real, tangible heightism, is what I always allowed to upset me most.

———————• ◆ •———————

Like most people, I always took great pride in taking personal responsibility for my actions.[36]

I always followed through with promises I made to others. Yet, when it came to taking care of my own mental health, I was the worst. It was different from taking responsibility for my actions.

Admitting I was depressed and sad meant I was a flawed human, and I wasn't willing to accept that premise.

For God's sake, I was a victim! I was only sad and depressed because people literally and metaphorically looked down on me. Because of that, I felt inadequate as a man.

But I have a dangly between my legs, and we with danglies aren't supposed to show signs of weakness or vulnerability.

---

36   It's not much different from everybody believing they are better drivers than everyone else. We all overestimate our own abilities.

I bought into that machismo when my dad died. I thought it was my responsibility to become a man the moment my mom told us the news. I asked her the night of his death if I could go to school the next day because men take care of their responsibilities.

From age seventeen through twenty-seven, I didn't cry a tear out of sadness or pain.[37] I cried briefly after my last high school football game and then held off until a tough romantic breakup a decade later. There were times I tried so hard not to cry that it made me vomit.

I bragged to my friends about my tear ducts' decade-long drought as if I'd won the Pulitzer. Because strength. Because Man.

I accepted I was depressed at age twenty-seven but blamed it on an unconfirmed chemical imbalance in my brain. Blaming it on a chemical imbalance allowed me to remain a victim because I had no control over something like that.

All I wanted was for something to take the pain away, so I got a family practitioner to prescribe fluoxetine, the generic for Prozac. If a little pill is all it took to get better, I was in!

It wasn't until I lost a customer service job because of my depression that I sought any sort of counseling.

Come to find out, counseling is only effective if you're honest with yourself and your therapist, which I wasn't. I'd already spent years forcing myself to believe I was a victim, and I refused to let go of that narrative even when I sat in front of someone who could help.

I continued the victim narrative, blaming not only that pesky little chemical imbalance for my depression but also my dad's death. I played the game for several therapists over the next couple of years, and I never went to the same one more than a handful of times or made it a priority to go consistently.

---

37   Not even third-degree rope burns from a rock-climbing incident could make the tears flow.

I tried acupuncture to cure my depression. It helped me feel physically better with some things, but it didn't address my real issues. When acupuncture and intermittent trips to therapists didn't magically fix me, I switched to a different antidepressant.

As divine intervention would have it, and unrelated to my depression, a friend of mine recommended attending a personal development seminar by Wings Seminars. I attended their Personal Effectiveness Seminar in April 2015, but the real game changer was attending their Crossover Seminar in January 2016.

In a group exercise, two fellow female participants used the word "small" while speaking to me. Although what they said was in no way a reflection of their thoughts about me, I chose to take offense and interpreted their words as a microaggression and an insult. [38]

While journaling about the experience that night, I had a soul-crushing "oh shiiit" moment. I realized I'd pissed away nearly two decades of life not taking responsibility for my feelings of inadequacy due to my height.

I slowly crawled out of my self-loathing mind-set, accepting the things I couldn't change about myself, and have been antidepressant free since July 2016.

I'm now okay with being short. Don't get me wrong; I'm not proud of it, but I'm not willing to allow my height to determine my identity anymore.

-------- ◆ --------

38   Due to signing a confidentially agreement with Wings Seminar, I cannot go into specific details about the exercises we did during the session. I was given permission to use this vague description for this book.

Choosing to play the victim is fucking stupid.

Case in point, a black man named Pedro Fequiere, a junior staff writer for Buzzfeed, wrote an article that appears to have two main titles. For reals. Visit the link in the footnote and tell me otherwise. Anyway, the second title was "I Dressed Up And Dressed Down For A Week As A Black Man And This Is How People Reacted."[39]

Buzzfeed is awful. They can eat shit and die.[40]

I was confused by the title of the article for two reasons. One, it's so poorly written that it's hard to take it seriously, and I thought it might be satire. Two, because I thought it could be satire, I wondered if it was written by a white man dressing up and down as a black man, and I thought, "How racist is *that*?"

Alas, the author is black.

Pedro starts his article with this: "I'm 24 years old, and like most black men my age I have to be extremely careful with what I choose to wear ... I don't want to be another statistic and have my appearance be the blame for it. But I won't conform and change my appearance just to make people feel more comfortable around me."

Pedro conducted a very simple social experiment. He dressed up for a week (blazers, slacks, ties, dress shoes) and dressed down for a week (hoodies, sweats, slippers) to gauge how people acted toward him.

To nobody's surprise, except maybe the author's, Pedro was treated with more respect and dignity and felt better about himself on the days he dressed up, which is true for anyone, not just a black man. He described dressing up as "cool" and that he "felt fancy."

---

39 Pedro Fequiere, "A Black Man Wore Different Kinds Of Clothing To See If People Treated Him Differently," *Buzzfeed*, March 8, 2016, https://www.buzzfeed.com/pedrofequiere/i-dressed-up-and-dressed-down-for-a-week-and-this-is-what-ha
40 #Buzzfeedcaneatshitanddie

Contrast that to the days he dressed down: "I mentally prepared myself for the microaggressions I was going to experience during my morning routine while reminding myself to act as I normally would."[41]

At the end of his experiment, he wrote this:

> But why does a woman need to protect her belongings from me in broad daylight? Why must it be for an interview if I'm dressed up? Why does a group of retail associates need to divert all their attention to me when I'm in a hoodie? Or why do they feel I'm more approachable with my shirt tucked in? I don't know, but I shouldn't have to change what I'm wearing not to be feared.

To answer Pedro: Because people unfortunately judge others based on their physical characteristics and how they present themselves.

Besides, I guarantee Pedro judges others based on how they look and present themselves. As humans, it's nearly impossible not to. We know from his essay that he judges people based on how he perceives them to judge him.

Even though he experienced the benefits of dressing up — and claims to *fear for his life* because of the way he dresses — he doesn't want to dress up after the experiment.

He proved to himself that he has an amazing power to help change the way others perceive him, but he chooses to give up that power because of the way he believes others should behave toward him.

By choosing not to dress up, he's setting himself up to experience additional discrimination because he idealistically believes society should be different from what it is.

---

41 Again, this is confusing because is he experiencing microaggressions during his morning routine, or is he mentally preparing himself during his morning routine? Fucking Buzzfeed.

Pedro is actively choosing to remain a victim, and his mind-set is more symptomatic of people today than ever before.

Like Pedro, when I was entrenched in my VM, I felt it was up to others, those I had no control over, to change and see me the way I wanted them to. Like Pedro, I left myself little personal power, as I put the onus on everybody else.

He's unwilling to change while expecting everybody else to change. He thinks he shouldn't have to change to feel comfortable even though he's disinclined to change for others to feel comfortable around him. Pedro wants society to bend to his rules and is unwilling to ditch the VM and take some personal responsibility in the matter.

It takes work to get out of the VM, Pedro. I promise you, it's totally worth it.

If you've discovered something that you indicate could help save your life, why wouldn't you take advantage of it and use it?

———————•◆•———————

Game Time! Answers

What's Happening in This Scene?

Of course, I was the bald, white man sitting alone at the bar. It was summer, and because I sweat a lot in the heat, I wore a black Five Four Club T-shirt with a snake on it (not a "Don't Tread on Me" shirt) to hide the horrendous pit wetness.[42]

---

42 The Equal Employment Opportunity Commission (EEOC) ruled in 2016, the year of this incident, that the Gadsden flag (the coiled snake with the "Don't Tread on Me" wording) could be considered racial harassment. Given the racial and political tension of that year due to the 2016 presidential election, it's likely the couple thought the bald white guy staring them down was racial harassment. Noah Feldman, "When a Flag Crosses the Line to Harassment," *Bloomberg,* August 5, 2016, https://www.bloomberg.com/view/articles/2016-08-05/eeoc-harassment-ruling-on-gadsden-flag-is-right

DONT TREAD ON ME

And I was high as fuck on a marijuana edible.

The black-bearded man looked like NBA basketball player James Harden. I couldn't remember his name and thought it would come to me if I snuck a few glances his way to jog my memory. I'm stoic; my normal countenance can be described as "resting dick face" (the male equivalent of "resting bitch face"), and I can only imagine how serious I looked as I concentrated on trying to recall who he looked like.

The last time I glanced over, they stared me down. I can only guess, but it didn't look like the kind of stare-down where they worried about my well-being or wanted to invite me over to their place later for drinks.

We're talking hate lasers.

Again, I can only guess, but the hate lasers they threw at me suggested this was war. They were ready to eviscerate the racist little turd who kept glaring their way because they were a mixed couple, and that type of intolerance just isn't cool, man.

I wanted to do so many things in that moment. I wanted to crawl up inside my own asshole and hide. I also wanted to buy them dinner because that always smooths things over, right? And I wanted to explain that I'm not racist, but that wouldn't have worked because I could barely say thank-you to the bartender when I paid my tab. So I did the only thing I could do, which was leave, because I was under pressure and not handling it well.

Again, I can only guess, but if they perceived me as a racist little turd, they chalked it up as another example of racism running rampant in society today when in fact no racism was intended at all.

Does He or Doesn't He Take Offense?

I took offense, all right. What sort of snot-rag says something as belittling as "Hey, big guy, what'll it be?" I wanted to punch his face.

I ordered my movie-time usual, which at the time was a Dr. Pepper and Sour Patch Kids. After receiving my soda, I struggled to get the paper wrapping off the straw, so I moved to the side as he took the next guy's order.

Snot-rag was at it again. "Hey, big guy, what'll it be?" I turned around, and the big guy he was helping was, well, a six-foot gent with a baseball cap.

I took offense for no reason. It was his go-to customer service line, which I understood because I was in customer service too. Had I not struggled with the wet straw wrapper, I would have chalked it up as another instance of blatant heightism.

He Considered *That* a Microaggression?

I chalked up the laughter of the hottie college women as a microaggression — and mean-spiritedness. Why else would they wait until I left the tableside to laugh? Because they were *obviously* laughing at how short I was.

My little ol' insecure self was unable to consider that maybe they were laughing at an inside joke, maybe they were just having a fun, giggle-inducing time. Maybe they were stoned. Maybe they were impressed with my service and thought I was cute. They could have been laughing at any number of things, but I *felt* they were laughing at me.

In that moment, I couldn't see it any other way.

I allowed the incident to affect my confidence for weeks. I allowed myself to believe most attractive college women were awful, and I was nothing but a little server boy for them to laugh at.

Looking back, of course, there's no good reason for me to have thought they were laughing at me. But that's the power a VM and perceived microaggressions have over people.

Pop Quiz

Sadly, the question I posed, "What would you do if you saw a banana peel in a tree?" wasn't a riddle.

If you're part of the University of Mississippi's Greek Life community, you could be triggered into thinking it's some sort of racist threat.[43]

While on a fraternity/sorority community retreat, a student put a banana peel in a tree instead of throwing it on the ground or waiting until he could properly throw it away. Three black students saw the peel dangling on the branch and interpreted it as a racist attack. The retreat was canceled because students didn't feel safe enough to stay.

They somehow linked the banana to racial lynching threats.

The VM makes you jump to insane conclusions about the intent of just about any scenario.

Their interpretation of the threatening banana peel is some next-level VM gymnastics, so kudos to their creativity, I suppose. However, this begs the questions: Would it have been any better had they found the banana peel on a sidewalk curb? Wouldn't that conjure up images of the curbside stomping scene in the movie *American History X*?

---

43   Slade Rand and Rachel Ishee, "Ole Miss Greek life retreat ends abruptly with bias concerns," *The Daily Mississippian,* August 30, 2017, http://thedmonline.com/greek-life-retreat-ends-abruptly-bias-concerns/

Also, what if they saw the banana peel in the garbage can? Wouldn't that have been like putting black people back into slavery and equating them to garbage?

Once you go down the VM road, you'll be able to see atrocities beyond your wildest dreams. You often have to make the mental leap from point A to point D to make it happen, but rest assured, you can interpret any incident to make yourself the victim in nearly every scenario.

Lies Hurt Real Victims

Whether or not you remember their names, you no doubt heard their distressing claims of racism or homophobia.

Michael Bennett of the Seattle Seahawks tweeted about a harrowing incident in Las Vegas after the McGregor/Mayweather fight in August 2017 when police were called to a casino because of an active shooter threat. Bennett claimed, among other things, "Las Vegas police officers singled me out and pointed their guns at me for doing nothing more than simply being a black man in the wrong place at the wrong time."[44]

Dauntarius Williams claimed someone wrote racist graffiti on his car at Kansas State University, which included the phrases "Go home n**** boy" and "Whites only."[45]

Baruch College student Yasmin Seweid claimed three white men attacked her on a Manhattan subway and tried to pull off her hijab while they screamed "Donald Trump!" and called her a terrorist.[46]

44 Jared Dubin, "Seahawks' Michael Bennett details harrowing story of racial profiling in Las Vegas," *CBS Sports,* September 6, 2017, https://www.cbssports.com/nfl/news/seahawks-michael-bennett-details-harrowing-story-of-racial-profiling-in-las-vegas/
45 "Kansas State Student's Car Vandalized – 'Go Home N****r Boy,'" *The Black Loop,* November 2, 2017, https://www.theblackloop.com/k-state-student-car-vandalized/
46 Andrew Buncombe, "Muslim woman says she was called a terrorist on New York Subway by three men chanting 'Donald Trump,'" *Independent,* December 4, 2016, https://www.independent.co.uk/news/world/americas/new-york-subway-muslim-woman-terrorist-donald-trump-yasmin-seweid-a7455336.html

Gay pastor Jordon Brown ordered a cake from Whole Foods, and instead of them writing "Love Wins" on it as he requested, he claimed they wrote "Love Wins Fag."[47]

The Air Force Academy was rocked with controversy when someone wrote outside a black cadet's room "Go home n*****." This prompted Lt. Gen. Jay Silveria to give a passionate speech against racism and bigotry in a video that went viral.[48]

All these incidents were lies.

About two hundred pieces of video evidence proved that Michael Bennett lied, as he crouched behind a gaming machine and then ran when police told him to get down. Everybody else was already obeying orders.[49]

Williams[50] and the black Air Force Academy cadet[51] wrote the threatening words themselves.

Pastor Brown wrote the word "fag" after he purchased the cake.[52]

And Seweid made up the entire hijab incident.[53]

---

47   "Austin pastor claims Whole Foods cake had homophobic slur," *CBS Austin*, April 18, 2016, https://cbsaustin.com/news/local/austin-pastor-claims-whole-foods-cake-had-homophobic-slur

48   Jamiles Lartey, "US air force academy chief delivers stirring speech telling racists to 'get out,'" *The Guardian*, September 29, 2017, https://www.theguardian.com/us-news/2017/sep/29/air-force-academy-general-racism-jay-silveria

49   Clay Travis, "Las Vegas Police Prove Michael Bennett Lied About Racism Charges," *Outkick The Coverage*, September 30, 2017, https://www.outkickthecoverage.com/las-vegas-police-prove-michael-bennett-lied-racism-charges/

50   Mara Rose Williams, "Racist graffiti painted on car near K-State was a fraud," *The Kansas City Star*, November 6, 2017, https://www.kansascity.com/news/local/article183086416.html

51   Anne Branigin, "Black Cadet Found Responsible for Racist Graffiti at Air Force Academy," *The Root*, November 8, 2017, https://www.theroot.com/black-cadet-found-responsible-for-racist-graffiti-at-ai-1820248614

52   Mike McPhate, "Gay Pastor Apologizes After Accusing Whole Foods of Writing Slur on Chocolate Cake," *The New York Times*, May 16, 2016, https://www.nytimes.com/2016/05/17/us/gay-pastor-apologizes-after-accusing-whole-foods-of-writing-slur-on-chocolate-cake.html

53   Christopher Mele, "Muslim Woman Made Up Hate Crime on Subway, Police Say," *The New York Times*, December 14, 2016, https://www.nytimes.com/2016/12/14/nyregion/manhattan-yasmin-seweid-false-hate-crime.html

These were all high-profile national headlines with little follow-up compared to the initial media reaction of outrage.

Lies hurt real victims.

Any excuse for lying is irrelevant because the endgame is the same: they all made themselves a victim because they wanted to be one — because victimhood is revered in society today.

Consider the impact the words that Bennett and Brown have on people. They are societal influencers. Professional athletes and pastors have voices that significantly influence the people who look up to them and see them as heroes. To have them lie about nonexistent discrimination fans the flames of societal tensions, hurting their overall cause instead of helping it.

If you think I'm blowing this problem out of proportion, consider research conducted by Sameer Hinduja, a professor of criminology at Florida Atlantic University and codirector of the Cyberbullying Research Center. He found about 6 percent of kids from the ages of twelve through seventeen have bullied themselves digitally.[54]

"It's a new phenomenon, and this is definitely happening for teens across the US," Hinduja said. "We have a tendency to demonize the aggressor, but in some cases, maybe one in twenty, the aggressor and target are the same."[55]

Kids are learning to make themselves the victims, and the victimhood culture will only continue to grow until we stop glorifying it.

———————— ◆ ————————

---

54   Sameer Hinduja, Ph.D., "Digital Self-Harm Among Adolescents," *Journal of Adolescent Health,* December 2017, https://www.jahonline.org/article/S1054-139X1730313-0/abstract

55   N'dea Yancey-Bragg, "Cyberbullying's chilling trend: Teens anonymously target themselves online, study finds," *USA Today,* November 8, 2017, https://www.usatoday.com/story/news/2017/11/08/cyberbullings-chilling-trenda-growing-number-teens-anonymously-bullying-themselves-online-study-find/831070001/

I'd like to end this chapter with the words of former Secretary of State Condoleezza Rice from an interview she did with *Motto* magazine:

> To be perfectly honest, I grew up in segregated Birmingham, Alabama, and that was macro-aggression, so I don't really get microaggressions. I grew up in a family where I was told you have to be twice as good. They said it as a matter of fact, not a matter of debate. They said there are no victims — the minute you think of yourself as a victim, you've given control of your life to someone else. I remember specifically my father saying once it's okay if someone doesn't want to sit next to you because you're black, as long as *they* move. So the message was don't let someone else's racism or sexism be your problem ... Now, if you're really denied something that you think you should have gotten, there are all kinds of means of recourse for that — and you ought to take them. But the everyday garden variety glance or interruption, you just can't let that get to you. You're just going to raise your blood pressure and be thrown off what you're really supposed to be focusing on.[56]

---

56   Lucy Feldman, "Condoleezza Rice: 'Don't Let Somebody Else's Racism or Sexism Be Your Problem,'" *Time,* June 28, 2017, http://time.com/4837393/condoleezza-rice-talks-racism-sexism/

CHAPTER 3:

The Dating

The trouble is not that I am single and likely to stay single,
but that I am lonely and likely to stay lonely.
— Charlotte Bronte

I had a huge crush on a five-foot-eight coworker while attending Boise State. During a fun shift together, we joked and flirted around, the fifties diner jukebox banging out hits of yesteryear. She looked me in the eyes, smiled sweetly, and said, "You know, if you weren't so short, I'd give you a chance."

I know women prefer taller men, but this was my first face-to-face encounter with the beast.

I would have been less humiliated had she pulled down my pants to my ankles while I took a customer's order. I stood there, plastic smile plastered on my face, while she sliced up my heart, used the ice cream shake blender to make a heart smoothie, and served it to me with a straw.

Suck that shit up, Bingham.

She told me I was quite the catch — enjoyable to be around, fun, witty, attractive, and worthy of love — except I stood a couple inches shorter, so I was not *really* worthy.

So I sucked that shit up. I pulled up my big-boy pants and dealt with it by pretending it didn't bother me, just as I'd trained myself to do since childhood.

Every time I log onto a dating application, I'm confronted with outspoken anti-short-man bias. Below is a fraction of a percentage of height discrimination examples I came across on Tinder and Bumble while trying to find someone to spend time with in 2016 and 2017.

31
Queen Mary, University of London
University of Fribourg
6 miles away

Applicants under 1.85 need not apply 😊

32
Western Oregon University
Western Oregon University
8 miles away

I'm an independent and outgoing person who loves to travel and be active. Looking for someone with a great sense of humor and will always join me on the dance floor.

Life's short, so you better not be.

29

7600 miles away

Living in Abu Dhabi, Road trip in the US soon.
Like Travel real men and music.
Hate cats and cities

Worst fear in life, waking up next to a short
metrosexual man who's wearing skinny jean.

33

12 miles away

LOVE HAS NO COLOR!!!!!   Loving Portland.... Looking for some cool people to hang with and continue
to see the city! !! Ready to try all of these adventures
natives are doing!! No kids just Me Me Me!!!! I love
Tequila and a nice sweet tasting cigar and a Tall man
to go with it!!! No hookups please!! I prefer meaninful
friendship!!! Im a US travelor, sorry guys not a World

40

 Location
Dollar Corner, Washington
22 miles away

 Info
An old soul, great morals, country girl, can dress to the 9's, clean
freak, business owner, hard working, great mother, huge sense
of humor, very independent, loves: sports, hunting, fishing,
hiking, golf, anything outdoors, coffee, etc. Non smoker, Im 5'8"
please don't LIE about your height OMG

40

Nurse
Linfield College, 2000

 Location
Hillsboro, Oregon
~27 miles away

 Info
Labor and delivery nurse, mom of 2, 5'7" and prefer men
6'-"ish" and taller... C'mon... no judgements please, I'm 5'10"
in heels;)
Enjoy witty, intelligent conversations, confident men
who have a sense of who they are and are open to the
possibilities of a relationship with a fantastic woman.

 37

Graphic Designer
Linfield College

 Location
Portland, Oregon
~11 miles away

 Info
ENFJ and tired of the dating scene. I'm not designed for
shallow relationships. Not looking for hookups. My "specs":
artist, singer, athlete, active, home owner, intelligent, pun
queen, no crazy exes, no kids, drama free, tall-ish. You:
stable, intelligent, fun, taller than me, athletic, non-smoker.

35
Deakin University

 Location
Lake Oswego, Oregon
16 miles away

 Info
I wish the men were as gorgeous as all the dogs and
babies!! 🐶 such a small town... soooo much facial hair lol!
I'm 5'10, if you're shorter than me please swipe left to save
us both some awkward texts and time... good luck! 😅 Oh
yeah, none of those ear hole things either, I just can't...!

33
University of Portland

 Location
Portland, Oregon
~12 miles away

 Info
I'm nice, patient, observant, smart, & funny. I enjoy being
active: boulding, xc skiing, jiu jitsu, etc.

My wit has nearly caused the death of a family member,
and also brought a boss to tears.

Looking for a LTR. Gold star if you're man-sized & do not
need to hide behind me in a wind storm.

 38

Naturopathic Physician at Self-Employed
National College of Natural Medicine, 2011

 Location
Portland, Oregon
7.8 miles away

 Info
Intelligent, emotionally intelligent, fit, driven, no drama.
Ready for LTR. May want kids. Conscious eater, bike
commuter, 5'8, home owner, chicken keeper, yoga, rock
climbing, camping, meditation. You: at least 5'8, intelligent,
mature, emotionally available, a force for good in the world.

Yes, in case you're wondering, you read that right: love has no color, just a height requirement. And so you know, I could log into Tinder right now and find you at least five more examples of anti-short men bias in the next ten minutes. It really is that prevalent.

Some women get angry when short men have the nerve to contact them. They see us as a tiny plague wreaking havoc in the online dating world, searching and swiping through profiles furiously with our angry little hands and ruining lives by daring to reach out to make a human connection with another human by writing things like "Hi, I enjoyed your profile and think your dog is adorable."

The horrors!

I've had many promising conversations with women until they ask me how tall I am. Because it's rude, I've never retaliated and asked them how much they weigh.

I'm not upset that women prefer taller men. Every human has the right to their preferences, and I would never wish to take those away from anybody. However, the outward disgust for short men falls outside the social norms of decency if compared to other marginalized groups.

Take the profiles above and switch the group of discrimination:

> Life is short, so you'd better not blow me up in a terrorist attack.

> I'm white; please don't lie about your ethnicity, OMG.

> I'm not handicapped. If you're not as mentally sharp as me, swipe left to save us both some awkward texts and time ... good luck!

> My worst fear in life is waking up next to a fat woman who wears skinny jeans.

> Blacks need not apply.

> Gold star if you're petite enough to stand behind me in a windstorm.

You may not have seen much wrong with what they originally wrote, but how do you feel now that you see it in another context?

Everybody has their preferences, but you rarely, if ever, see a profile specify preferences against other ethnic groups or that denigrate fat people. It's socially unacceptable to discriminate against those groups because we've been conditioned not to be outwardly bigoted toward them.

Short men do not receive the same considerations.

While most women get offended when a man doesn't want to date a fatty, those same women have no reservations about telling the world they would never date a shorty.

They don't comprehend it's almost the same prejudice. I say "almost" because shortness is a fixed state, whereas fatness, in most cases, is combatted by diet and exercise.

I can't change my height by changing my lifestyle choices.

Seeing constant reminders that I'm not desirable enough to date wasn't good for my mental well-being. I allowed their incessant dislike of short men to keep me depressed, bitter, and in a VM for years.

Ladies, is it too much to kindly request an end to the outward discrimination against short men in your profiles? You know, like we aren't supposed to rail against overweight women?

You've fought so hard for equality, why not try implementing your own standards?

Men are demonized if they post anti-fat women sentiments on a dating site. Take this story titled "Guy fat shames woman on Bumble, Bumble responds accordingly."

> Instead of anyone being able to message anyone, it's up to the woman to make the first move [on Bumble] — thus (hopefully) stemming the never-ending flow of creeps you tend to find on other dating apps.

> One thing that can make anyone feel pretty powerless, however, is being fat shamed.

> Which is exactly what happened to one woman on the app.

> And, just to add insult to injury, it was as he was simultaneously ghosting her.

> Submitting her story to *Elite Daily* column Boom, Ghosted, the woman said the two matched on Bumble and got on pretty well.

But after one seemingly good date, he stopped responding to her.

These things happen, right?

But it get (*sic*) worse.

The woman decided to get back on the dating horse, is scrolling through the app and finds the same guy with a new profile – this time there is one extra sentence: 'Pleeeeeeease don't be fat in real life.'

Oh, great.

Even if you had a thick skin to take this in stride (I sure wouldn't), this would be enough to make anyone angry.

Especially the fact that such an ar*e could exist on the app created to avoid situations like this.

Which is where the more positive side of the story comes in, because Bumble saw the article, tracked the guy down, and banned him.

And so, the feminist dating app lived up to its reputation, and dished out justice.[57]

An article on the *People* magazine website discusses the same incident:

"I know it could have been about someone else, but the coincidence is a little sketchy to me," the woman told Elite Daily. "So now, I want to publicly roast him for being a misogynistic pig. And by the way, I'm not actually fat. I can just squat, like, 200

---

57 Alice Sholl, "Guy fat shames woman on Bumble, Bumble responds accordingly," *Metro,* January 22, 2017, https://metro.co.uk/2017/01/22/guy-fat-shames-woman-on-bumble-bumble-responds-accordingly-6397888/

lbs., so I have pretty thick thighs."

Bumble's guidelines state that disrespectful behavior is not allowed, and clearly they are serious about protecting their users from any shaming comments.[58]

It's hard to explain what happened to my brain after reading about this incident, but I'll try. Imagine the Fourth of July fireworks over the Statue of Liberty. The crisp, clear night is lit up by reds, whites, blues, and purples, with the satisfying sound of the explosions in the distance. If you're close enough, you're lucky to smell the gorgeous, nostalgia-inducing firework smoke wafting gently all around you.

Now imagine someone lighting the fireworks simultaneously in the middle of the day in a sketchy back alley covered with bad graffiti. It's a never-ending barrage of high-intensity bangs and booms echoing off the back-alley walls, and no matter where you turn or how much pressure you put on your ears to dull the sound, you can't escape the thick blanket of noise and chaos surrounding you. All you can do is crawl to the nearest corner, curl up in the fetal position, bury your face in your knees, rock back and forth, and pray for it all to end before you lose your sanity. Or you could end it all by sacrificing yourself on a bundle of Roman candles and let sweet, sweet death take over.

She admitted his profile comment may have been about someone else, but her victim game is strong, and she *made* it about herself, so she felt justified to publicly shame him as a misogynistic pig.

That means we should all publicly shame women for being misandrist slum dogs when they body-shame short men.

Equality, am I right?

58   Gabrielle Olya, "Bumble Dating App Bans User for Fat-Shaming His Date," *People*, January 19, 2017, https://people.com/bodies/bumble-dating-app-bans-user-for-fat-shaming-his-date/

You don't suppose the misandrist slum dog I came across on Bumble who wrote, "Please don't LIE about your height, OMG," was in a similar situation as the pig who so brazenly wrote, "Pleeeeease don't be fat in real life," do you?

Stating a preference against fat women is the cardinal sin of dating. Yet, most women aren't introspective enough to understand they are doing the same thing to short men.

But why would they be? They have no reason to think short-shaming men is a thing because they're not taught it's wrong. They're taught to be the victims in these scenarios. It doesn't cross their mind they can be the victimizers.

Men are supposed to have thick skin. We're not allowed to let silly things like a height preference in a dating profile upset us.

If I were to get thousands of women banned from Bumble for being misandrist slum dogs because they body-shame short men, do you think anyone would write an article praising me for my bravery and indicating justice was served?[59]

It's frustrating for both men and women when others are dishonest on dating apps. I've been on many dates with women who've used profile photos from half a decade ago. In the summer of 2016, I had a date with an obese woman with a mustache who used profile pics from her college years that ended in 2010. None of her pics showed signs of obesity or a mustache.

Women lie about their weight/body type, and men lie about their height for the same reason: they are afraid others will disqualify them from consideration because of these characteristics.

The only difference is one is socially acceptable, whereas the other isn't. We're far more sympathetic toward women than men when it comes to body shaming. The Huffington Post and People.com have

---

59   Of course, the answer is no, but it would financially destroy Bumble.

body-shaming sections on their websites.[60] If you scroll through the stories, you'll notice the vast majority of body-shaming articles have to do with fat/skinny shaming against women.

Where are the stories on these sites about body-shaming short men?

As you'll see in a future chapter, the media isn't shy about short-shaming men, and they do it with glee.

Men are actually short-shamed all the time, and on prominent platforms.

Erica Morin, five foot ten and an assistant history professor at Westfield State University, somehow got a speaking gig for a Tedx Talks at TedxTexasTechUniversity titled "Female, Educated, and Perpetually Single."[61]

As the title suggests, Erica is perpetually single. Her list of thirty-six things she was looking for in a guy since childhood has dwindled to five. The number one thing on her list: "taller than me."

Number one!

Erica laments, "I don't care if it's superficial and shallow. I want some-body that's taller than me. I'm five foot ten; I am not a small girl, all right. I don't want somebody that's going to make me feel bigger than I already am." A few minutes later she has the nerve to say, "I'm keep-ing my eyes, my mind, and my heart open." And seconds after that, she continues, "And more than once, a circa five-foot-four, three-hun-dred-pound *dude* hitting on me ... which, like, looks aren't everything, and I applaud your confidence, buddy ... but really, *really?* Come on."

60 https://www.huffingtonpost.com/topic/body-shaming and https://people.com/tag/body-shaming/
61 Erica Morin, "Female, educated, and perpetually single," published February 19, 2014, at TedxTexasTechUniversity, Lubbock, TX, video, 11:35, https://www.youtube.com/watch?v=dE8UHCDVYB8&t=395s

If you watch that far, I hope you at least get a little sickened by her condescending sarcasm when she applauds the confidence of short, obese men as if they are less of a human being than she is.

Erica carefully laid out this speech for broadcasting to the world, and that's how she chose to short and fat-shame men. It's despicable.

But what would you expect from a vacuous windbag who references Buzzfeed in a Tedx speech?[62]

If she said any of these things about another marginalized group, or another woman, she would be unemployable.

Some men are intimidated by taller women and wouldn't consider dating them. While it's irrelevant in Erica's case, as she automatically dismisses men because they happen to be shorter than her, research suggests women are more likely to reject men than the other way around.

Alison Denisco wrote this for the Huffington Post:

> How do tall women and short men survive in the dating world? A 2008 study of 382 undergraduates in the journal *Personality and Individual Differences* found that both sexes preferred relationships where the woman was shorter than the man. Curiously, the research also showed that women enforced the norm more strongly than men. Twenty three percent of men but only four percent of women said they were open to a relationship in which the woman was taller.
>
> "Women's cultural vision is being feminine, having a man big enough to make her feel protected. Many women hold this stereotype to a point where it excludes a lot of people they might be interested in otherwise," said Dr. Pepper Schwartz, a sociology professor at the University of Washington in Seattle, and the chief relationship expert for PerfectMatch.com.[63]

---

62   #Buzzfeedcaneatshitanddie
63   Alison DeNisco, "Dating: Women May Care More Than Men Who's Taller," *Huffington Post,*

Another study published in the *Journal of Family Issues* states that 48.9 percent of women restricted their online dating searches to men who were taller than them, whereas just 13.5 percent of men said they would not consider a taller woman.[64]

Does anybody else find it amusing that Erica's complaining about her own shallowness? The average height for men in America is five feet nine. She automatically rejects over half the men in the country because she's admittedly superficial. That's cool, that's Big E's choice, but to then complain to us that she's still single based on her own choices and prejudices is astonishing. That's like a white supremacist complaining he can't find a suitable bride in Africa.

She's a victim of her own making and got a Tedx Talk out of the deal.

What are the chances a man in a Tedx Talk could ever complain about being single by saying, "I don't care if it's superficial and shallow, I want someone smaller than me. I'm five-eleven, ripped, and don't want someone who's going to dwarf me with her obesity and make me look less fit than I am … I'm totes keeping an open mind and shit, yet more than once a five-foot-one, sausage-fingered little piggy who weighs at least two hundred fifty pounds has the audacity to contact *me?* I mean, come *on.* Looks aren't everything, I suppose. Kudos on your confidence, I guess."

He'd never get a speaking gig again, and Bumble would take swift action and block him from using its service for his douchebaggery.

And America would rejoice.

Think about this: Pining for a taller man goes against most tenets of modern-day feminism. Feminists don't need men, and they most certainly wouldn't worry about feeling protected, smaller, or awkward

updated July 18, 2012, https://www.huffingtonpost.com/alison-denisco/dating-women-men-whos-taller_b_1527117.html

64   George Yancey and Michael O. Emerson, "Does Height Matter? An Examination of Height Preference in Romantic Coupling," *Journal of Family Issues,* 2014, https://pdfs.semanticscholar.org/529f/b5c2aef307e6eddf0c9ab19ba192192f9f45.pdf

with a shorter guy, right? Isn't having a taller man the evil patriarch's vision of what coupledom should look like?

Feminist Kate Whittle wrote:

> "He's a nice guy. But he's, like, two inches shorter than me."

> Heard that before, either from a friend or your own mouth? I am a feminist, but as a heterosexual woman I prefer to date guys who are taller than me. I'm not the only one. I've automatically dismissed many a potential date because he was shorter than me. Various studies say women in general prefer tall guys, and attribute it to evolutionary preference for big, healthy, protective males.

> It's a dilemma. I don't believe in any of that patriarchal "he-man" protector crap. I'm an independent woman and I support myself. I certainly don't need some six-foot muscular hunk to protect me from bears.

> A big part of my height preference is, of course, what I've unconsciously absorbed from society. I grew up with the standard Disney princess model of relationships. Disney princesses do not marry the short guy. Hetero couples where the man is shorter often get mocked. I'm ashamed that the thought "If I marry a short guy, I can't wear heels on my wedding day" has actually gone through my mind. I don't even plan on getting married.[65]

According to a *Washington Post* survey in early 2016, six in ten women in America identified as a feminist.[66] Women, fight against the evil patriarchy and date a short man *now*! Show them who's boss!

---

65 Kate Whittle, "Sorry, Man, You're Too Short (Am I A Bad Feminist?)," *Ms. Magazine,* May 27, 2010, http://msmagazine.com/blog/2010/05/27/sorry-man-youre-too-short-am-i-a-bad-feminist/
66 Weiyi Cai and Scott Clement, "What Americans think about feminism today," *The Washington Post,* January 27, 2016, https://www.washingtonpost.com/graphics/national/feminism-project/poll/

Yet I digress.

According to a *New York Post* article, the dating site AYI.com (now FirstMet.com) conducted a study of New York City area women and their willingness to date shorter men. They found that in Manhattan and the Bronx, women respond to men under five foot nine 1.2 percent of the time. In Brooklyn, it's 2.4 percent; Staten Island, 4.1 percent; and Queens is at 5.4 percent. In Jersey City, the women are obviously crazy, as they respond 7.6 percent of the time.[67]

That's not very feminist of y'all.

Wanna know what else isn't very feminist? Dating short men only if they make a lot of money.

Duke professor and researcher Dan Ariely conducted a study about online dating and found that for every inch a man was under five foot ten, he had to make $40,000 more per year to be as successful in the dating pool as his taller peers.[68]

That means if I'm up against gym teacher Gary, who is five foot ten, and he makes $50,000 per year, I'd have to make $250,000 per year to be as desirable as Gary, who probably has jock itch, ringworm, an alcohol problem, and a crush on the head cheerleader.

You'll be hard-pressed to find anyone who hasn't likened dating to job hunting. Now that online dating is mainstream, dating profiles are like job applications.

The National Bureau of Economic Research (NBER) conducted a study to gauge race discrimination against minorities in the job market. The bureau found that "job applicants with white names needed to send

---

67   Gary Buiso, "Short men don't stack up with NYC women," *New York Post,* December 8, 2013, https://nypost.com/2013/12/08/short-men-dont-stack-up-with-nyc-women/
68   Olivia Zhu, "Advice in the 'Love Market' from Dan Ariely," *Duke Research Blog,* February 11, 2014, https://researchblog.duke.edu/2014/02/11/advice-in-the-love-market-from-dan-ariely/

about 10 resumes to get one callback; those with African-American names needed to send around 15 resumes to get one callback."[69]

At its base level, how is the discrimination that women have against short men any different from the discrimination some potential employers may have against minority applicants?

Women are far more prejudiced against short men than some potential employers are of minority job applicants.

Let that sink in.

Social justice advocates use the 50 percent disparity of callbacks to minority candidates for a job as proof of systemic racism.

Why, then, wouldn't we consider women's refusal to reply to or date short men as systemic heightism?

Of course, that would mean we would have to hold ourselves to the same standards as we expect from others, but, as you'll see later, that's not something we're really interested in. We claim to all want equality, but as it is, we want others to treat us differently, not necessarily that we'll treat others equally as well.

We're so undesirable and systemically oppressed, sperm banks don't even accept our deposits!

From the *Men's Journal* website, one thing that can eliminate you from consideration for being a sperm donor is your height:

> Following insights from supply and demand, California Cryobank doesn't take on donors who have a BMI outside the normal range. Among white donors, they also require their donors to be taller than 5'10". For other ethnicities, including Hispanic and Asian, the height requirement is less stringent because there are fewer applicants. [Scott Brown, director

---

69   David R. Francis, "Employers' Replies to Racial Names," *The National Bureau of Economic Research,* http://www.nber.org/digest/sep03/w9873.html

of client experience at California Cryobank] has heard of additional limitations from other banks, including redheads. California Cryobank doesn't have that rule because they want a diverse donor pool. "You want to have as complete a catalog as possible and have as many options [as possible] for people," Brown says. They usually have about 525 donors to choose from at any time.[70]

They want as complete a catalog with as many options as possible ... except they exclude over half the male population to achieve said "complete catalog."

Imagine going into a sperm bank to donate, but instead of ensuring you're over five foot ten, they pull out their Crayola Multicultural Crayon pack, and if your skin is darker than "tan," you're turned away. Many would say that is systemic racism and white supremacy in action, a sign that society doesn't value darker shades of skin.

As it is, women who do not want to date shorter men or do not want a shorter sperm donor are only seen as voicing a personal preference, so it's nothing to worry about.

Anyway, according to sperm banks and the clientele they serve, I'm among the least desirable of men on earth because I'm short and ginger.

It's a good thing I'll be rich once this book is published.

———— ◆ ————

It's rare, but I've had great dates with taller women.

Upon meeting a five-foot-nine woman from Tinder for drinks, the first words out of her mouth were "Wow, you're short."[71]

70 Taylor Kubota, "8 Reasons Your Sperm Isn't Good Enough to Donate," *Men's Journal*, https://www.mensjournal.com/health-fitness/9-reasons-your-sperm-isnt-good-enough-to-donate-w209421/
71 What are the chances she ever would have said, "Wow, you're black," or "Wow, you're fat"?

Wow indeed.

She held a lit cigarette between her pointer and middle finger. I would have been completely justified in replying, "Is your soul as black as your lungs must be?"

Because I'm not an asshole, I said, "I guess you didn't vet me as well as you should have."

She felt awful, which is good; it's the right way to feel after saying shitty things. She was apologetic and embarrassed.

After the initial awkwardness, we ended up having a great night together. When I drove her back to her car at three in the morning, she offered kindly, sincerely, and unexpectedly that as a date, she rated me an eight out of ten.

Folks, an eight out of ten on a Tinder date is exceptional, even though we mutually agreed we weren't interested in a relationship with each other.

I smiled because she would never have gone out with me had she known she was four inches taller than I was.

Many of us never get a chance to show someone how much we can offer them. Women dismiss us shorties with regularity and then lament, "Where are all the good guys?" and "Why am I still single?"

We may literally be right under your nose.

———— ◆ ————

But shorties, not all is hopeless. We do have at least one feminist ally out there.

Zero, zero chance.

I'll end this chapter with some words from Ann Friedman, who wrote an article for *Esquire* magazine that said in part:

> The first question most strangers ask me is "How tall are you?" If I'm feeling charitable, I answer honestly: "6-foot-2." They often follow-up with, "Do you ever date shorter men?" Consider this my full answer.
>
> First off: Yes, I have. Which makes me weird. The average woman is eight percent shorter than her male partner. In one survey, about half of collegiate men required their date to be shorter, while a monstrous nine of every ten women said they would only date a taller man. And online, it's even more brutal: Women can calculate how tall they are in their highest heels, add a few inches for good measure, and then filter out men who fall below that sum. Of course the ability to search for people who meet our criteria is part of the appeal of online dating. But while women say they have a "type" — they love bearded gingers or get off on guys in glasses — they don't filter out *every* man who doesn't meet those specific physical criteria. Height is different. It's a sweeping prejudice masquerading as a sexual preference. When one guy changed his height on his OkCupid profile from his actual 5'4" to an average 5'9", his response rate nearly doubled.
>
> This is bullshit. Single people sign up for a half-dozen dating sites and apps in order to widen their pool, yet most won't break the height taboo. It needs to change. Men should date women who are taller than they are, and women should date shorter men. For chrissakes [sic], I'm talking about *all* of us getting laid here! Only four percent of heterosexual couples feature a shorter man. Let's increase our odds.
>
> Everyone, it is time to expect more. To go on even just one date with someone who falls outside our eight-percent range,

and to ask ourselves whether there's actually less chemistry there. To think of a world with all these new, gorgeous options. If you won't do it for yourself, try it for my sake. I'd really appreciate if we could stop asking "How tall are you?" We're above it.[72]

---

72 Ann Friedman, "Why Shorter Men Should Go After Taller Women," *Esquire,* December 11, 2013, https://www.esquire.com/lifestyle/sex/a26348/date-a-taller-woman/

CHAPTER 4:

The Media

I believe the most important thing for the media is to be objective, fair, and balanced. We should not report a story with preconceptions or prejudice.
— Jack Ma, cofounder and chair of Alibaba Group

The 2016 presidential election pitted the two least likable candidates in election history against each other: Hillary Clinton at five foot four versus Donald Trump at six foot three.[73]

Despite the height difference, they're both colossal assholes.

As the shorter candidate, Clinton was paranoid. According to the _New York Daily News_:

> The Democratic nominee, who is 5-foot-4, has apparently enlisted the help of a raised podium for the first presidential debate against Donald Trump, who is 6-foot-3, Monday night, photos of the two podiums show.
>
> According to WABC's Rita Cosby, one of the two podiums inside the debate hall at Hofstra University, in Hempstead, NY,

---

73 Alvin Chang, "How tall are Hillary Clinton and Donald Trump compared to you?" _Vox_, Updated October 19, 2016, https://www.vox.com/debates/2016/9/26/13063118/how-tall-hillary-clinton-donald-trump

is larger than the other.

It is believed that the larger one was built at Clinton's request to make her appear taller than she is.

"Clinton is 5'4" and Trump 6'2" and her team wanted the podium modified or a box added so she won't look short next to Trump," Cosby said in an email.[74]

The national media also did her a huge favor by broadcasting the debates in a split screen so the height difference wasn't noticeable.

Candidates have worried about height differences before, as the issue came up in 1976 with Carter versus Ford, as well as in 1988 with Dukakis versus Bush.

Tom Murse, in an article on the website thoughtco.com, wrote this:

During one of the Republican presidential debates before the 2016 election, the web search company Google tracked what terms Internet users were searching for while watching TV. The results were surprising.

The top search wasn't *ISIS*. It wasn't *Barack Obama's last day*. It wasn't *tax plans*.

It was: How tall is Jeb Bush?

The search analytics unearthed a curious fascination among the voting public: Americans, as it turns out, are fascinated with how tall the presidential candidates are.

It's true: Taller presidential candidates have fared better through

74 Adam Edelman, "Hillary Clinton to use larger podium than Donald Trump at first debate to make up for height disadvantage: report," *New York Daily News,* September 25, 2016, http://www.nydailynews.com/news/politics/clinton-debate-podium-larger-trump-report-article-1.2805846

history. They haven't always won. But they were victorious in a majority of elections and the popular vote about two-thirds of the time, according to Gregg R. Murray, a Texas Tech University scientist.

Murray's analysis concluded that the taller of the two major-party candidates from 1789 to 2012 won 58 percent of the presidential elections and received the majority of the popular vote in 67 percent of those elections.[75]

It's not just Americans who are obsessed with height when it comes to political leaders. Former French President Nicolas Sarkozy received negative headlines for being a five-foot-five man. He is also famous for marrying former model Carla Bruni, who is five foot nine.

From the *International Business Times*:

A recent column in Britain's *Daily Telegraph* newspaper described Sarkozy and Berlusconi as "pygmies."

Sarkozy's midget-like height has long been discussed in European media. Reportedly, he is extremely sensitive about his small stature and reacts angrily to any aspersions about his tiny frame.

In March 2010, Cameron [David Cameron, 6-foot-1 Prime Minister of Great Britain] allegedly made a remark about "hidden dwarfs" when discussing a photograph of himself and Sarkozy.[76]

Marvel at this gem from nbcnews.com:

75 Tom Murse, "Why Height and Physical Stature Play a Role in American Politics," *ThoughtCo,* Updated July 9, 2017, https://www.thoughtco.com/does-the-tallest-presidential-candidate-win-3367512
76 Palash Ghosh, "Sarkozy, Berlusconi and Medvedev: The Long and the Short of it," *International Business Times,* October 29, 2011, https://www.ibtimes.com/sarkozy-berlusconi-medvedev-long-short-it-212673

From elevator shoes to step-up boxes behind podiums, and even his own tippy toes, Nicolas Sarkozy and his handlers have tried to compensate for his height — or lack thereof.

Now, a factory worker's claim that she was chosen to stand near the French president during a photo shoot because she is short is making waves on the Internet — and rankling Sarkozy's office.

The brouhaha was sparked during a visit to an auto parts plant in Normandy last week in which Sarkozy laid out his support for industry and defended his controversial plan for a "carbon tax" to help the environment.[77]

His height causes brouhahas! I love that word! Now every time I hear it I'll think of little Nicolas and all the international ridicule he caused himself for being my height. Silly little man should know better.

Other headlines range from "Does Nicolas Sarkozy have short-man syndrome?" and "Why does President Sarkozy go to such ridiculous lengths to disguise his true height?" to "A tall tale! 5'5" Nicolas Sarkozy is ridiculed after beach photographs emerge that make him appear TALLER than statuesque wife Carla Bruni."

Short men are in a lose-lose situation when it comes to, well, simply being ourselves. On one hand, we're ridiculed for our height, or as nbcnews.com so eloquently put it, our "lack thereof." On the other hand, if we try to look taller by using elevator shoes or boxes behind podiums, or choose to stand next to someone close to our own height, we are ridiculed yet again, and the media are like alcoholics in a liquor store, excited and ready to pounce and delegitimize us at the drop of a beer cap.

---

77   "France's Sarkozy using short people as props?" *NBC News,* September 8, 2009, http://www.nbcnews.com/id/32739805/ns/world_news-europe/t/frances-sarkozy-using-short-people-props/#.W67JxuhKjIU

Then they can get their *brew*hahas at our expense.[78]

Also note the stark contrast in how the media writes about Sarkozy as opposed to Clinton for nearly identical tactics of trying to look taller. The articles about Clinton are factual and objective.

But the media is eager to take jabs at every opportunity when it comes to Sarkozy, as they question whether he has short-man syndrome, and say he has midget-like height, he goes to ridiculous lengths to hide his shortness, and he causes commotions for wanting to stand next to someone his height.

Even respected fellow media members can't catch a break from their own kind when it comes to short shaming.

The celebrity news website Page Six ran this in July 2017:

> George Stephanopoulos may be a giant in the news business, but *Good Morning America* has changed its set to cover up his diminutive size.
>
> "He's 5-foot-6 and is dwarfed by human trees Robin Roberts and Michael Strahan," says an insider. "'GMA' initially thought using an anchor desk with elevated chairs would help the problem. Still awkward, George's little-boyish mini-legs were seen dangling."
>
> So a month ago, a silver panel was added across from the anchor desk at midlevel, covering up where Stephanopoulos' feet rested on his chair, which up to then had been "visible and awkward."
>
> Reportedly, Stephanopoulos is 5-foot-7, Roberts is 5-foot-10, and Strahan is a whopping 6-foot-5. Height has been an ongoing issue on the ABC show.

---

78   Get it?

Back in 2011, there were rumors Stephanopoulos could be swapped out after network execs liked the way 6-foot-3 Josh Elliot looked next to Roberts.

In 2010, Page Six reported that ABC staffers were gossiping that Roberts continued to wear high heels to tower over Stephanopoulos as a "sign of power."

But George's wife, Ali Wentworth, has no problem with her husband's stature, having said, "He's 5-foot-7. But 6-foot-7 in bed!"[79]

This is not parody.

It's incomprehensible that someone would write an article about how visible and awkward it is to have Robin Roberts on the set of GMA, that the amount of melanin in her skin has been an ongoing issue for the show, that they were going to swap her out because execs liked the way fair-skinned Josh Elliott looked next to Stephanopoulos, or that Stephanopoulos wore a white hoodie around her as a "sign of power." But don't worry, it's all good, because Robin's partner has no problem with her race, and even reports, "She's as white as the virgin snow in bed!"

The media is complicit in perpetuating stereotypes about short men. They help perpetuate notions that short men aren't adequate providers, but rather bumbling idiots who are no more than old children and can't help but have a complex about their shortness.

DirecTV had a run of commercials with celebrities and NFL players to push its NFL Sunday Ticket package in 2014. One of them was titled "Petit Randy Moss."[80] The commercial assumes short men make bad

---

79   Mara Siegler, "How 'GMA' hides George Stephanopoulos' 'little-boyish mini-legs,'" *Page Six,* July 12, 2017, https://pagesix.com/2017/07/12/how-gma-hides-george-stephanopoulos-little-boyish-mini-legs/
80   "Petite Randy Moss Commercial" published August 30, 2015, video, 0:31, https://www.youtube.

life decisions, are uptight (as portrayed by the way he dresses), are imbeciles, and are overall bitter because their favorite cereal is on the top shelf.

Kudos to DirecTV for getting so many clichés crammed into one thirty-second spot.

Many people complained about the unfair depiction of short men. So DirecTV did what any reputable company would do after offending a large swath of their audience, which was to write a public apology and pull the ad.

Ha! Kidding!

Here's what DirecTV told *Adweek*: "Randy Moss was one of the tallest receivers to play the game, which of course is a joke. Besides, these ads obviously take place in an alternate reality, something our viewers understand. The feedback we're getting is the vast majority enjoy them."[81]

Companies pull ads and apologize for offending their customers quite frequently, vast majority be damned. But unlike DirecTV, other companies *actually apologize and pull their ads!*

Shea Moisture, a personal care company, released a promotional video on its Facebook page. It showed a blond woman complaining about her straight hair, as well as another white woman saying she felt pressure to dye her hair blond.

Seems innocent enough. Except, you see, there were no black women in the ad, and many black women complained about it.

Shea Moisture responded, "Wow, okay — so guys, listen, we really f-ed this one up. Please know that our intention was not — and would

com/watch?v=2guO5bNqCOY

81 David Gianatasio, "'Petite Randy Moss' is Cable's Latest Victim in DirecTV's New Height-Mocking Ad," *Adweek,* August 25, 2015, https://www.adweek.com/creativity/petite-randy-moss-cables-latest-victim-directvs-new-height-mocking-ad-166535/

never be — to disrespect our community, and as such, we are pulling this piece immediately because it does not represent what we intended to communicate."[82]

Pepsi pulled an ad featuring Kylie Jenner because it was accused of using the Black Lives Matter movement to sell its products. The company responded, "Pepsi was trying to project a global message of unity, peace, and understanding. Clearly, we missed the mark and apologize. We are pulling the content and halting any further rollout."[83]

Coca-Cola apologized for sexist Sprite ads that ran on the Irish men's lifestyle site JOE.ie. The ads, part of its #BrutallyRefreshing campaign, contained lines such as "You're not popular, you're easy," and "She's seen more ceilings than Michelangelo." Coke responded, "We're sorry for any offense caused by the #BrutallyRefreshing Sprite campaign in Ireland, which was intended to provide an edgy but humorous take on a range of situations ... We recognize that on this particular occasion the content did not meet this standard and we apologize."[84]

Want more? Check out these apologies from Nivea,[85] McDonalds,[86] PopChips,[87] and Burger King.[88]

---

82   Shea Moisture, Facebook, April 24, 2017, https://www.facebook.com/SheaMoisture/posts/wow-okay-so-guys-listen-we-really-f-ed-this-one-up-please-know-that-our-intentio/1495966387121658/

83   Douglas Quenqua, "Pepsi says 'sorry' and removes Kendall Jenner ad from the web," *PR Week,* April 5, 2017, https://www.prweek.com/article/1429761/pepsi-says-sorry-removes-kendall-jenner-ad-web

84   Andrew Alexander, "Sprite: 'Brutally refreshing' — or sexist?" *BBC News,* August 3, 2016, https://www.bbc.com/news/world-europe-36958158

85   Tracy Saelinger, "Nivea apologizes for 'White Is Purity' ad campaign after outrage," *Today,* April 6, 2017, https://www.today.com/style/nivea-apologizes-white-purity-ad-campaign-after-outrage-t110066

86   Ashley May, "McDonald's apologizes for 'insensitive' UK ad about child coping with father's death," *USA Today,* May 16, 2017, https://www.usatoday.com/story/news/nation-now/2017/05/16/mcdonalds-apologizes-insensitive-uk-ad-child-coping-fathers-death/324549001/

87   Sheila Marikar, "Ashton Kutcher's Popchips Ad Pulled After Racism Outcry," *ABC News,* May 3, 2012, https://abcnews.go.com/blogs/entertainment/2012/05/ashton-kutchers-popchips-ad-pulled-after-racist-outcry/

88   "Burger King Apologizes For Controversial Commercial," *Popsugar,* April 15, 2009, https://www.popsugar.com/food/Burger-King-Apologizes-Controversial-Commercial-3036005

Snickers pulled an ad that ran during the Super Bowl in 2007 where two mechanics ate a Snickers bar from each end, concluding with them touching lips. Gay rights organizations condemned the commercial as homophobic, arguing the men's reactions (tearing out their own chest hair to prove their manliness) demeaned gay men.[89]

However, Snickers ran an ad for its Snickers Bites product that read, "Smaller size. No inferiority complex." The company never responded to complaints about perpetuating the small person/inferiority complex stereotype, and of course it never pulled the ad.

We're in a world where it's not okay to offend the protected classes, even if there's no intention to offend. Companies fall all over themselves to apologize for offending minorities, women, and homosexuals, yet they don't care about offending short men.

Of course, there are plenty of instances in the television and movie industries perpetuating short men stereotypes. Just think Lord Farquaad in *Shrek*, Percy in *The Green Mile*, or George Costanza in *Seinfeld*.

How often are you aware when a short man is shorter than their fellow costars (unless their character is depicted as the stereotypical angry/doofus/childish/worthy-to-be-made-fun-of short guy)?

Tom Cruise, five foot seven, is often shown next to his fellow six-foot actors as the same height. There's no way Ethan Hunt could do all his heroics in the Mission: Impossible series if he were smaller. How laughable!

Cruise also plays the role of Jack Reacher. In the novels, Reacher is six foot five and 220 pounds, with a fifty-inch chest. From the *Los Angeles Times* website, Reacher fans were not impressed with the choice of actor:

"I WAS going to see it. I am SOOO in lust with Reacher. So

---

89   Paul Farhi, "Mars Scraps Snickers Ad After Complaints," *Washington Post,* February 7, 2007, http://www.washingtonpost.com/wp-dyn/content/article/2007/02/06/AR2007020601871.html

when I saw the trailer I was SOOO disappointed. Cruise is NOT Reacher. Channing Tatum IS. I cannot believe they actually used an arrogant overexposed short IMBECILE to create such an awesome character. I will not see it and it literally RUINED the whole character for me. HOW COULD THEY DO THIS?" — Melody Overland

"I totally agree with every other fan that is saying Tom Cruise IS NOT Jack Reacher. I am so upset that they chose Tom to play this role. I will not pay money to see this movie, either. Get a real man to play that role and I will be the first in line to see the movie." — Laura Seager

"It appears that I am not the only one who believes that Cruise is too short, too small, and too old. Even the best of actors (which Cruise is not) would not be able to overcome these handicaps." – Jere Seibert

"WHY have you ruined Jack Reacher for all of Childs' fans? YOU'RE TOOOOOO SHORT AND TOOOOOOO OLD!!!" – Lynn Timon[90]

Lee Child, author of the Jack Reacher books, said, "Reacher's size in the books is a metaphor for an unstoppable force, which Cruise portrays in his own way." He was excited that Cruise was cast to play the role.

That doesn't stop people from hating Cruise for being short. There was even a Facebook group with over ten thousand likes and 9,800 followers where fans posted comments about his height:

"Cruise has ruined my ability to read any further Reacher books. My mental picture will be of a miniature putz instead of

---

90   Carolyn Kellogg, "Reader reactions to 'Jack Reacher': The fans are furious," *Los Angeles Times*, December 21, 2012, http://www.latimes.com/books/jacketcopy/la-et-jc-tom-cruise-jack-reacher-fans-react-20121220-story.html

a powerhouse enforcer."

"How could some weedy little ex-pretty boy play our big, tough, gentle, dependable Jack Reacher?"[91]

Fans of certain franchises are always angry at some casting choices for one reason or another. Take Ben Affleck as Batman, Scarlett Johansson in *Ghost in the Shell*, Daniel Craig as James Bond, and Hugh Jackman as Wolverine.

However, Reacher fans are personally angry at Cruise, in large part because he's short. They resort to ad hominem attacks, calling him arrogant, an imbecile, and a miniature putz, and portraying him as undependable, which are all common short-men stereotypes.[92]

Cruise gets crucified all the time for his height. The media love to point out that his ex-wives Nicole Kidman and Katie Holmes are taller.

The taller-woman/shorter-man celebrity couples are never safe from unjust criticism. Sophie Dahl is five feet eleven, and her husband, Jamie Cullum, is five foot four. From the *Daily Mail*:

> In pictures, it always looks as though Jamie, a jazz pianist and singer, has been digitally shrunk by a third, or that Sophie has been elongated by the same degree … Jamie, meanwhile resembles an escapee from Lilliput, the land of the little people in Jonathan Swift's *Gulliver's Travels*.[93] (Residents of Lilliput are six inches tall.)

Jamie wears cowboy boots in one of the photos, which prompts the passage, "Even in the cowboy boots he's taken to wearing to make up the difference, he can't get past her shoulder." Apparently, a short

---

91   Tom Cruise is not Jack Reacher, https://www.facebook.com/reacherfriends/
92   I just hope everyone who hates Cruise because he's short realize he'll always be more successful than them.
93   Natalie Clarke, "Little and large: Why Sophie Dahl and Jamie Cullum think their height difference is no big deal," *Daily Mail*, June 17, 2009, https://www.dailymail.co.uk/femail/article-1192162/Little-large-Why-Sophie-Dahl-Jamie-Cullum-think-height-difference-big-deal.html

man cannot wear a pair of fashionable cowboy boots unless he's trying to make up a height difference.

Tall men don't need an excuse to wear cowboy boots.

Where's the article about George Lucas and his wife, Mellody Hobson, in which they say their race difference is not a big deal, wherein Hobson wears a white dress to try to be as white as Lucas, and she's said to look as if she came from Pierre Boulle's novel *Planet of the Apes?*

It doesn't exist because it's too racist, offensive, and gross to make those comparisons. Anyone writing that would rightfully lose their job and be unhirable forevermore.

Case in point, the Roseanne Barr tweet that said, "muslim brotherhood & planet of the apes had a baby=vj" which I referenced at the beginning of this book. ABC immediately canceled Barr's sitcom, *Roseanne*, the network's hit show, and talent agency ICM dropped her as a client, saying it was "distressed by the disgraceful and unacceptable tweet."[94]

Take the drivel from Buzzfeed[95] videos titled "Badass Facts You Didn't Know About Tall People," which was published in late 2016.[96]

When I get offended by something heightist, my reaction anymore is generally mild, such as "Wow, that's heightist," and I'm good at letting it go. When I saw this video, however, I felt like shoving shit down the throats of everyone at Buzzfeed and watching them die of suffocation.

How's that for playing the stereotypical angry short man?

94   Rebecca Sun, "Roseanne Barr Dropped by ICM Partners After Racist Tweet," *Hollywood Reporter,* May 29, 2018, https://www.hollywoodreporter.com/news/roseanne-barr-dropped-by-icm-partners-racist-tweet-1115460
95   #Buzzfeedcaneatshitanddie
96   "Badass Facts You Didn't Know About Tall People," Published November 30, 2016, Video, 1:29, https://www.youtube.com/watch?v=4vhNiaCp5w8

Besides being triggered immediately by the awful, tinny beats, the first thing we see are the words "Taller people could be smarter!" Yes, with an exclamation point!

Thirty-three seconds in, we are still subject to the shitty music but also the caption that says, "Tall people also tend to make more money," with a very punchable dude dancing some asshole money dance, probably on the graves of short men who died poor.

Pray do tell, in what world would it be remotely okay to say that white people are smarter than blacks, or rejoice in dance while proclaiming men make more money than women? All the while calling these things "badass."

Take your time. In the meantime, the next chapter awaits.

CHAPTER 5:

The Wage Gaps

Life is not easy for any of us. But what of that? We must have perseverance and above all confidence in ourselves. We must believe that we are gifted for something, and that this thing, at whatever cost, must be attained.
— Marie Curie

Whether you think you can, or you think you can't – you're right.
— Henry Ford

What a difference six years makes.

April 17, 2012, was Equal Pay Day. This is a yearly schtick, so don't worry if you missed it this last time around; you'll have another chance to be outraged next year.

On that day, The Young Turks, a politically progressive YouTube news channel, took the time to discuss the gender wage gap. Anchors Ana Kasparian and Cenk Uygur lamented as follows:

> Ana: Today is Equal Pay Day, and Equal Pay Day symbolizes how far into 2012 women have to work to earn the same salary

that men earned in 2011. It gives you an idea [that] there's a little bit of a disparity when it comes to how much men get paid versus how much women get paid. To give you exact numbers, and this was reported by the Associated Press, it'll take about forty-five years to eradicate this wage gap. In 1967, women earned fifty-eight cents to every man's dollar. In 2010, women only earned seventy-seven cents to every man's dollar.

Companies want to get away with paying as little as possible to their employees, and if they know that the law protects them from paying women less than men, then they're going to continue to do that because at the end they are looking at their bottom line. Of course, I think maybe sexism has a role to play in this as well, but profits have a much larger role in this than anything else, in my opinion.

And also, another thing is companies will always make the same argument: Welllll, women are gonna take time off because they're gonna have a baby; they're not as profitable, na na na na naaaaa.

Cenk: Na na na na naaaaa, na na na na naaaaaaa.....

Ana: And also keep in mind, this is on average, so there are of course isolated incidents throughout the country where women are making more than men at any given company, but when you look at the big picture, women are still only making seventy-seven cents to every man's dollar.[97]

Two things to note. One, the law does not protect companies for paying women less than men. The Equal Pay Act of 1963 makes that illegal.[98] And two, "na na na na naaaaa" are not words. Using nonwords

---

97 The Young Turks, "Equal Pay Day and the Wage Gap," Published April 17, 2012, Video, 4:45, https://www.youtube.com/watch?v=WqCuMHcLiPQ

98 "The Equal Pay Act of 1963," *U.S. Equal Employment Opportunity Commission*, https://www.

and a sarcastic tone to try to dismiss legitimate and true arguments means you have no coherent response to said argument.

Let's jump ahead six years to April 15, 2018. The Young Turks got another opportunity to talk about the gender pay gap:

> Ana: The Census Bureau has just released a *fascinating* look into when women have children and how much it negatively impacts the gender gap between them and their husbands. Now the most interesting part of the study was that if women have these children before twenty-five or after thirty-five, they're much more likely to close the gender (pay) gap with their husbands.
>
> The study found that immediately after the birth of the first child in the marriage, the pay gap between spouses doubles, entirely driven by a drop in the mother's pay. Men's wages, though, keep rising because they don't necessarily have to deal with the disruption of having that baby. Usually with the child-rearing, the bulk of the work, even now with more equality, lands or falls on the mother. When women have their first child between the ages of twenty-five and thirty-five, their pay never recovers relative to that of their husbands.

Cenk correctly points out that these years are the prime years to both have a family and establish a career. He also admits that, at the heart of the story, it explains a lot regarding the reasons for the gender pay gap.

Ana continues:

> Even in families in which both parents work full time, women spend almost double the time on housework and childcare. And when women work fewer hours, they are paid disproportionately less and become less likely to get raises and

---

eeoc.gov/laws/statutes/epa.cfm

promotions. So when women have children during that time frame, keep in mind that they inevitably will have to dedicate more of their time to raising their kids, and as a result they are not able to work around the clock as women who don't have children can do.

By the way, I did some digging. Go check what the current gender wage gap is, and even though people throw around that statistic of I think it's seventy-seven cents to the dollar, the reality is, if you compare the same jobs that men and women are working, you're comparing apples to apples, the gender pay gap has shrunk considerably, women earning ninety-eight cents for every dollar that men earn.

Cenk: This is illuminating in finding out what one of the issues is. It doesn't mean that there isn't bias against women. One of the parts of the study that I found most interesting is even if the woman was making more than the man in the relationship, she was the one that was expected to take care of the baby, or did in reality take care of the baby, and then that hurt her earning potential significantly in the twenty-five- to thirty-five-year range. And so the family actually lost more money than if the husband stayed at home and taken care of the kids. But on average, *they didn't*; it was the woman who stayed home and took care of the kids. And a lot of those choices are voluntary; they're not based on bias or societal expectations. Some women want to stay home and take care of their children. That's perfectly normal and understandable. But are there also societal expectations? Yes.[99]

As more studies emerge, it's becoming clearer that child-rearing and other personal choices account for most, if not all, of the gender wage

99   The Young Turks, "Key To Women's Pay Gap Discovered," Published April 15, 2018, Video, 8:58, https://www.youtube.com/watch?v=TL7ajQzpyWg

gap. So now, instead of blaming workplace discrimination, proponents of the pay-disparity narrative have shifted their argument that societal expectations, or "structural factors," are to blame for the gap.

Among those structural factors? Women's occupational choices are shaped by discrimination and social norms, the culture of male-dominated industries (which generally pay higher) are a huge turnoff to women, and extreme job pressure that "disproportionately rewards those able to work brutally long hours and be on call 24/7."[100]

Harvard economist Claudia Goldin, in a 2014 study, indicates, "The gender gap in pay would be considerably reduced and might vanish altogether if firms did not have an incentive to disproportionately reward individuals who labored long hours and worked particular hours."[101]

Of course, this information has been around since at least 2009, yet the "women are victims" narrative persists. Christina Hoff Sommers, a resident scholar at the American Enterprise Institute (AEI), where she studies the politics of gender and feminism, and a former philosophy professor at Clark University, wrote this:

> The AAUW (American Association of University Women) has now joined ranks with serious economists who find that when you control for relevant differences between men and women (occupations, college majors, length of time in the workplace) the wage gap narrows to the point of vanishing. The 23-cent gap is simply the average difference between the earnings of men and women employed "full time." What is important is the "adjusted" wage gap – the figure that controls for all the relevant variables. That is what the new AAUW study explores.

---

100 Kathleen Geier, "The Gender Wage Gap Is Not Women's Fault, and Here's the Report That Proves It," *Rewire News,* July 27, 2016, https://rewire.news/article/2016/07/27/wage-gap-not-womens-fault-heres-report-proves/

101 Claudia Goldin, "A Grand Gender Convergence: Its Last Chapter," *American Economic Review,* 2014, https://scholar.harvard.edu/goldin/publications/grand-gender-convergence-its-last-chapter

The AAUW researchers looked at male and female college graduates one year after graduation. After controlling for several relevant factors (though some were left out, as we shall see), they found that the wage gap narrowed to only 6.6 cents. How much of that is attributable to discrimination? As AAUW spokesperson Lisa Maatz candidly said in an NPR interview, "We are still trying to figure that out."

One of the best studies on the wage gap was released in 2009 by the U.S. Department of Labor. It examined more than 50 peer-reviewed papers and concluded that the 23-cent wage gap "may be almost entirely the result of individual choices being made by both male and female workers." In the past, women's groups have ignored or explained away such findings.

Women's groups will counter that even if most of the wage gap can be explained by women's choices, those choices are not truly free. Women who major in sociology rather than economics, or who choose family-friendly jobs over those that pay better but offer less flexibility, may be compelled by cultural stereotypes. According to the National Organization for Women (NOW), powerful sexist stereotypes "steer" women and men "toward different education, training, and career paths" and family roles. But are American women really as much in thrall to stereotypes as their feminist protectors claim? Aren't women capable of understanding their real preference and making decisions for themselves? NOW needs to show, not dogmatically assert, that women's choices are not free. And it needs to explain why, by contrast, the life choices it promotes are the authentic ones — what women truly want, and what will make them happier and more fulfilled.[102]

102 Christina Hoff Sommers, "Wage Gap Myth Exposed – by Feminists," *Huffington Post,* November 4, 2012, https://www.huffingtonpost.com/christina-hoff-sommers/wage-gap_b_2073804.html

Along the same lines as they must *show* rather than just *assert* that women's choices are not free, they should also have to *show* rather than just *assert* that employers are discriminating against women when it comes to pay disparity.

Just because there's a disparity in something doesn't mean it's the result of discrimination.

Case in point: In 2016, 69.7 percent of NFL players[103] and 74.3 percent of NBA players were black,[104] yet blacks only comprise 13.4 percent of the population (which means black men only comprise between 6 to 7 percent of the population).[105] No rational person would proclaim this inequality is because of discrimination on the part of the employers.

It's unfortunate that I must make myself clear here because many of you are branding me a misogynistic pig and want to choke me right about now, but I am for equal pay for equal work if everything is indeed equal.

I also understand there are forms of workplace discrimination that may affect women more than men, such as unwanted sexual discrimination. However, I don't think that contributes to *pay* disparity. They are separate issues.

The fact that, on average, self-employed women make less than self-employed men also hurts the narrative that employer discrimination plays a significant role in the wage gap. The reasons for the self-employed pay gap are the same as before: men and women choose to start businesses in different industries, and self-employed women work fewer hours than self-employed men.[106]

---

103   Richard Lapchick, "The 2016 Racial and Gender Report Card: National Football League," *The Institute for Diversity and Ethics in Sport,* September 28, 2016, http://nebula.wsimg.com/1abf2 1ec51fd8dafbecfc2e0319a6091?AccessKeyId=DAC3A56D8FB782449D2A&disposition=0&allow origin=1

104   Marc J. Spears, "Where Are All the White American NBA Players?" *The Undefeated,* October 25, 2016, https://theundefeated.com/features/white-american-nba-players/

105   United States Census Bureau, July 1, 2017, https://www.census.gov/quickfacts/fact/table/US/PST045217

106   "The Gender Gap in Self-Employment and Hiring," *Pew Research Center,* October 22, 2015,

Additionally, even in the "gig economy," women are making 7 percent less than men. And wouldn't you know it, I'm starting to sound like a broken record, but it's all based on women's choices:

> A recent study of Uber drivers found a big pay gap. The participating economists – two from Uber, two from Stanford, and one from the University of Chicago – looked at data from a million of the independent drivers who had worked for the company.
>
> They found a 7 percent difference in earnings between men and women. The result surprised the researchers given the algorithmic nature of the fare assignments.
>
> You might wonder at the assumption algorithms are gender blind given that research has shown computer code, written by people, can be biased by race, gender, or class. In this case, the researchers said that gender isn't even collected as a factor.
>
> Instead, here's what they said caused the difference in earnings: "We find that the entire gender gap is caused by three factors: experience on the platform (learning by doing), preferences over where/when to work, and preferences for driving speed. This suggests that, as the gig economy grows and brings more flexibility in employment, women's relatively high opportunity cost of non-paid-work time and gender-based preference differences can perpetuate a gender earnings gap even in the absence of discrimination."[107]

I also think there's an overlooked aspect to the wage gap: a lack of confidence on the part of women. But don't take my word for it.

---

http://www.pewsocialtrends.org/2015/10/22/the-gender-gap-in-self-employment-and-hiring/

107 Erik Sherman, "Women Make Less As Uber Drivers And That's Bad News For The Gig Economy," *Forbes,* February 10, 2018, https://www.forbes.com/sites/eriksherman/2018/02/10/women-make-less-as-uber-drivers-and-thats-bad-news-for-the-gig-economy/#61ae7503560e

Take it from Katty Kay and Claire Shipman, authors of the book *The Confidence Code for Girls*, who wrote this in an article for *The Atlantic*:

> Even as our understanding of confidence expanded, however, we found that our original suspicion was dead-on: there *is* a particular crisis for women – a vast confidence gap that separates the sexes. Compared with men, women don't consider themselves as ready for promotions, they predict they'll do worse on tests, and they generally underestimate their abilities. This disparity stems from factors ranging from upbringing to biology.
>
> A growing body of evidence shows just how devastating this lack of confidence can be. Success, it turns out, correlates just as closely with confidence as it does with competence. No wonder that women, despite all our progress, are still woefully underrepresented at the highest levels. All of that is the bad news. The good news is that with work, confidence can be acquired. Which means that the confidence gap can be closed ...
>
> Talking with [Washington State University psychologist Joyce] Ehrlinger, we are reminded of something Hewlett-Packard discovered several years ago, when it was trying to figure out how to get more women into top management positions. A review of personnel records found that women working at HP applied for a promotion only when they believed they met 100 percent of the qualifications listed for the job. Men were happy to apply when they thought they could meet 60 percent of the job requirements. At HP, and in study after study, the data confirm what we instinctively know. Underqualified and underprepared men don't think twice about leaning in. Overqualified and overprepared, too many women still hold back. Women feel confident only when they are perfect. Or practically perfect ...
>
> We were curious to find out whether male managers were

aware of a confidence gap between male and female employees. And indeed, when we raised the notion with a number of
male executives who supervised women, they expressed enor-
mous frustration. They said they believed a lack of confidence
was fundamentally holding back women at their companies,
but they had shied away from saying anything, because they
were terrified of sounding sexist. One male senior partner at
a law firm told us the story of a young female associate who
was excellent in every respect, except that she didn't speak
up in client meetings. His takeaway was that she wasn't confident enough to handle the client's account. But he didn't know
how to raise the issue without causing offense. He eventually concluded that confidence should be a formal part of the
performance-review process, because it is such an important
aspect of doing business.[108]

So what does any of this have to do with heightism?

The gender wage gap isn't the only wage gap game in town.

Short men (and overweight women) tend to make less than their
taller (and thinner) counterparts. And I believe it comes down to one
main choice: confidence.

Travis Bradberry, author of the book *Emotional Intelligence 2.0*, wrote
on the *Forbes* website:

> I think Henry Ford said it best: "Whether you think you can,
> or you think you can't – you're right." Ford's notion that your
> mentality has a powerful effect upon your ability to succeed is
> manifest in the results of a recent study at the University of
> Melbourne where confident people went on to earn higher
> wages and get promoted more quickly than anyone else.[109]

---

108 Katty Kay and Claire Shipman, "The Confidence Gap," *The Atlantic*, May 2014, https://www.
theatlantic.com/magazine/archive/2014/05/the-confidence-gap/359815/

109 Travis Bradberry, "12 Things Truly Confident People Do Differently," *Forbes*, April 1, 2015,
https://www.forbes.com/sites/travisbradberry/2015/04/01/12-things-truly-confident-people-do-

Joe Pinsker from *The Atlantic* wrote:

> In the 1960s and 70s, Thomas Gregor, an anthropologist at Vanderbilt, traveled to central Brazil to see if height was prized by people beyond the developed world. For years, he observed the Mehinaku, a group that lived in the tropical forest and was so thoroughly unmodern that they had never seen eyeglasses. He spent time with the Navajo and the Trobriand Islanders of Papua New Guinea, too. "In no case," he would later write, "have I found a preference for short men."

> The bias that George showed to be embedded into human social life plays out quantifiably in the professional world: In Western countries, a jump from the 25th percentile of height to the 75th – about four or five inches – is associated with an increase in salary between 9 and 15 percent. Another analysis suggests that an extra inch is worth almost $800 a year in elevated earnings. "If you take this over the course of a 30-year career and compound it," one researcher told Malcolm Gladwell for his book *Blink*, "we're talking about a tall person enjoying literally hundreds of thousands of dollars of earnings advantage."

> It used to make sense that height would be valued when picking people to do jobs: The tallest people were often the biggest and strongest, and most tasks demanded size and strength. But the height premium has persisted even as more and more jobs have become desk jobs. Economists have sought a satisfactory explanation ever since that change started taking hold....

> Some studies suggested that taller people have better social skills and more self-confidence ("noncognitive" skills, as academics would say). People who were taller as children, the thinking goes, were treated better, so they developed more

differently/#79a0f4864766

emotional stability, which has been shown to help on the job. Meanwhile, other studies have found that taller people are inherently smarter: As early as age three, they do better on aptitude tests.[110]

From Business Insider:

The body you are dealt with in life is a strong predictor of whether you will find wealth or poverty.

Scientists have long known there is a link between body size and wealth but assumed that poorer people didn't grow as tall or were not as healthy because of bad nutrition.

New researchers at the University of Exeter in the UK have found strong evidence that being a shorter man or more over-weight woman leads to fewer chances in life, including lower income.

The study of 120,000 people, published in the British medical journal BMJ, came to some stark conclusions.

Men who are 7.5 cm shorter on average, purely because of genetics, earn about 1,500 British pounds ($2,800) a year less than others.

Similarly, if a woman is 6.3 kg heavier for no other reason than her genetics then this means her income is 1,500 British pounds ($2,800) a year less than a comparable woman of the same height who is lighter.

"This is the best available evidence to indicate your height or weight can directly influence your earnings and other

---

110 Joe Pinsker, "The Financial Perks of Being Tall," *The Atlantic,* May 18, 2015, https://www.the-atlantic.com/business/archive/2015/05/the-financial-perks-of-being-tall/393518/

socioeconomic factors throughout your life," says Professor Tim Frayling of the University of Exeter Medical School.

This won't apply in every case, many shorter men and over-weight women are very successful, but science must now ask why we are seeing this pattern.

"Is it down to factors such as low self-esteem or depression, or is it more to do with discrimination?"

The researchers say shorter height leads to lower levels of education, lower job status, and less income, particularly in men.

A range of factors could link taller stature to a higher social position although this study did not look at which factors.

However, the researchers say possibilities include complex interactions between self-esteem, stigma, positive discrimination and increased intelligence.

"These findings have important social and health implications, supporting evidence that overweight people, especially women, are at a disadvantage and that taller people, especially men, are at an advantage," they write.[111]

From the website Talent Culture:

It would be downright bizarre if employees were being rewarded directly for their height. But perhaps they are being rewarded for a personality trait that often comes as a side effect of increased stature: confidence.[112]

---

111 "Science says you'll make less money if you are short and fat," *Business Insider Australia,* March 8, 2016, https://www.businessinsider.com/science-says-youll-make-less-money-if-you-are-short-and-fat-2016-3
112 Simon Davies, "Is Taller Better? Explaining the Height Wealth Gap," *Talent Culture,* May 2, 2017, https://talentculture.com/taller-better-explaining-height-wealth-gap/

I'll give you a second, but have you noticed anything about the articles on the height wage gap that would cause outrage if spoken about another marginalized group?

Claiming that short people are less intelligent is one thing. Calling it "downright bizarre" for employees to pay short men less is another.

It's not socially acceptable to claim that blacks or women are less intelligent than their counterparts, even if these claims are backed up by science. These studies are always called "controversial"[113] or say that the science is "bogus" or "debunked."[114]

It's so socially unacceptable that Charles Murray, in his 1994 book *The Bell Curve,* found that there were differences of intelligence between ethnicities, and he's still branded a racist and sparks protests when he is invited to speak on college campuses.[115]

These scientific test results are always controversial when they indicate anything negative about some marginalized group, yet they appear to be scientifically sound if results are negative about short men. Yet, if short men make less money than their taller peers in part due to lower intelligence, wouldn't it stand to reason the same would apply to women and blacks?[116]

Additionally, nobody would call it "downright bizarre" for employees to pay women or blacks less. That would be called "institutional discrimination."

I'm going to make a controversial statement right now: Many women are more privileged than men when it comes to the workforce, and I think the wage gap is proof of that.

---

113 Jeanna Bryner, "Men Smarter than Women, Scientist Claims," *Live Science,* September 8, 2006, https://www.livescience.com/7154-men-smarter-women-scientist-claims.html

114 Gavin Evans, "The unwelcome revival of 'race science,'" *The Guardian,* March 2, 2018, https://www.theguardian.com/news/2018/mar/02/the-unwelcome-revival-of-race-science

115 Laura Krantz, "'Bell Curve' author attacked by protestors at Middlebury College," *Boston Globe,* March 5, 2017, https://www.bostonglobe.com/metro/2017/03/04/middlebury/hAf-pAIHquh7DISIdoiKbhJ/story.html

116 Yes, it does, but saying that would make me sexist and racist, so I'm definitely not saying that.

I think child-rearing is more important than a formal job. I think if you have the means and will to put your career on hold and start a family, you're going about life the right way, and you should take advantage of that any way you can. I don't think success should be determined by our wages or earnings, and I certainly don't think anyone has said while on their deathbed that they wished they had spent more time at work.[117]

Like Big Erica in chapter 3 complaining that she's single because of her own biases, I think some women are complaining they make less because they've chosen to live a more fulfilling life outside the confines of work. Those are downright bizarre things to complain about.

But of course, what do I know? I'm just a short whitey with a dangly between my legs. How *dare* I have such a wrong opinion on one of the most important issues of our lifetime!

Yet I digress again …

Confidence is a choice. If short men make less money because they lack confidence, that's their own fault, and they have nobody to blame but themselves.

I'm certainly not going to blame an employer for promoting a taller, more confident man over a shorter, less confident one. I'd do the same thing. I'm not going to promote a person I don't have confidence in, and people who don't have confidence in themselves do not instill confidence in others.

I have no doubt that the lack of confidence in many short men is directly attributed to the discrimination they encounter in other aspects of their daily lives.

---

117 Bronnie Ware, "Regrets of the Dying," https://bronnieware.com/blog/regrets-of-the-dying/

CHAPTER 6:

The Undesirables

People have said I have the Napoleon complex. But I've always had to fight for everything that I have.
— Chris Paul

I was very short when I was little, so I probably had — and there may be a residue of it now — that Napoleon complex. Wanting to be as big and as powerful as the big guys.
—Wesley Snipes

I am a man with Down syndrome and my life is worth living.
— Frank Stephens

According to encyclopedia.com, the "Napoleon complex refers to a specific type of inferiority complex associated with short people, and especially with short men ... Individuals with this disposition are claimed to overcompensate for their short stature by being excessively belligerent, hostile, or quarrelsome in their interpersonal relationships ... However, the Napoleon complex is said to motivate other forms of behavior besides interpersonal violence and aggression. Most innocuously, a short male might make himself feel taller by placing home wall hangings a little lower than normal. Or he might wear shoes with thicker heels."[118]

We can all agree that's a broad definition of a mental condition.

We should also all agree the NC doesn't exist unless people discriminate against short men. Why would short men feel the need to overcompensate unless they are led to feel that they have to?

Most people have heard of the NC and attribute it to short men, but at the same time they scoff at the concept of heightism.

That's illogical.

I have no doubt the NC is real for many short men. It's one of those unfortunate stereotypes that is true for a reason. It will continue to be a problem until the discrimination against short men ends.

How often have you accused, either secretly or to his face, a short man of having the NC?

Short man works out? Must have the NC. Short man has a nice car? Dude's obviously overcompensating and must have the NC. Short man lost his temper? Little bro, stop being so sensitive, tall men never lose their temper!

Did you know every time you attribute the NC to a short man you're attributing to him a mental disorder?

Try that with another group and a different ailment. I triple-dog dare you.[119]

Go ahead, accuse an upset woman of having PMS, you sexist monster.

Ever accuse a gay man of having AIDS after he sneezed?

---

118 Thomas Gale, "Napoleon Complex," *Encylopedia.com,* 2008, https://www.encyclopedia.com/social-sciences/applied-and-social-sciences-magazines/napoleon-complex

119 No time to go through the normal single- or double-dog dare; I skip straight to the triple.

When was the last time you told the fat guy his diabetes could be cured if he just stayed away from the desserts?

Hell, it's even considered rude to assume a pregnant woman is pregnant.

It's unacceptable to diagnose someone else's health, either mental or physical. Yet unqualified individuals diagnose short men as having the NC all the time, and nobody thinks twice about it.

And dear lord, generalizing that short men wear shoes with thick soles or hang pictures lower is a symptom of the NC? Are you fucking kidding me?

What's the equivalent mental disorder for women who wear heels or don't want to strain their necks while looking at art in their own living rooms?

It's a deplorable double standard that helps perpetuate heightism, especially as the lack of repercussions embolden some to diagnose the mental health of short men.

Of course, if you tell me I have short-man syndrome and I get upset at your fallacy, it's just proof that I do have it, right?

While it's unacceptable to diagnose our mental health for any negative reactions we have, it exists in many as an unfortunate result of discrimination, which is a main factor in the mental health issues we face.

I've already mentioned my depression and VM because of discrimination. But it can get much worse for some of us, and nobody should take it lightly.

From Vice.com:

> Recent research on military men at Camp Pendleton showed an increased risk of depression for the guys who stood 5'8" and below. Valery Krupnik, the clinician at the helm of the study,

stated that the physical demands of a career in the military likely play a role in these cases of depression. "When people find themselves outliers for reasons beyond their control, like physical attributes, they face a challenge in addition to all the challenges average people face," Krupnik told LiveScience.com.

As for civilians, the data doesn't paint a pretty picture either. The average male in the United States, according to the CDC, stands just over 5'9". Those falling below that benchmark will face a variety of hurdles, ranging from career prospects to dating partners, all of which can plummet a guy's self-esteem.

Daniel Freeman, a clinical psychologist at Oxford who has studied the effect of height on paranoia, told me that among those who are taller, "the chances of feeling anxious or depressed tend to be a little lower. Greater height is also associated with a slightly lower risk of suicide."

In fact, for every two inch increase in height in men, the risk of suicide goes down 9 percent, according to a Swedish study published in the *American Journal of Psychiatry*. Even after controlling for socioeconomic status, education level, and prenatal factors, the researchers still found a "twofold higher risk of suicide in short men than tall men."[120]

Lisa Hitchen wrote on the *New Scientist* website that males born short have two and a half times the risk of attempting suicide than average-length babies:

Violent deaths were defined as hanging, shooting, cutting, jumping from a height or in front of a moving vehicle, drowning, or intentionally crashing.

---

120 Justin Caffier, "Science Says Being Short Makes You Depressed," *Vice,* October 19, 2015, https://www.vice.com/en_us/article/7bd7jb/it-sucks-to-be-a-short-guy-511

The team found both that males born measuring less than 47 centimeters, and those of low birth weight (below 2.5 kilograms or 5.5 pounds) presented a similar risk of a violent suicide attempt. Whilst being born preterm (before 34 weeks) increased the risk over four-fold.[121]

According to the American Foundation for Suicide Prevention, white males accounted for seven of ten suicides in 2016 in the United States.[122] The CDC indicates males of all races accounted for 77.9 percent of all suicides. [123]

The psychological issues don't stop at depression. Enter paranoia.

Jason and Daniel Freeman (mentioned in the *Vice* article above) wanted to find out the psychological consequences of feeling smaller than usual. They conducted an experiment with sixty women and put them through a virtual reality simulation:

> The participants took the virtual tube journey twice: once at normal height and once with their perspective altered to mimic how the scene would look if they were about a head's height shorter (the order of the journeys was randomized). The results were dramatic: when they felt smaller, the participants reported increased feelings of inferiority, weakness, and incompetence. And this explained why they were also more likely to experience paranoid thoughts: for example, that someone in the carriage was being hostile or trying to upset them by staring.
>
> We didn't tell the participants that we'd lowered their height, and very few noticed. "It felt different in the two times. I felt

121 Lisa Hitchen, "Men born short are more prone to violent suicide," *New Scientist*, January 17, 2008, https://www.newscientist.com/article/dn13196-men-born-short-are-more-prone-to-violent-suicide/
122 "Suicide Statistics," *American Foundation for Suicide Prevention*, https://afsp.org/about-suicide/suicide-statistics/
123 "Suicide: Facts at a Glance," *Centers for Disease Control*, 2015, https://www.cdc.gov/violenceprevention/pdf/suicide-datasheet-a.pdf

more vulnerable the first time [lowered condition], and also the man with the legs in the aisle was acting in a hostile way towards me the first time, but I didn't feel it so much the second time, even though his legs were in the same place, I don't know why!" was a typical comment. Another participant remarked: "I felt more intimidated the first time [lowered condition], not sure why. There was a girl who kept putting her hand to her face, the man with the blue T-shirt was shaking his head at me, they were staring at me more."[124]

Hello again, dear friend microaggressions. When in the lowered condition, many of the participants felt they were on the receiving end of microaggressive behavior whereas in the higher condition they didn't.

Virtual reality characters have no hostile intention, so it's illogical that the man with the legs in the aisle is an asshole in only one scenario.

Short people face other issues in crowded areas.

In 1980, *The Journal of Social Psychology* published a study:

> Ninety-one male and female adults, who were walking in the corridor of a commuter train station situated in a large metropolitan area of the United States, were given the option of violating the personal space of either a tall or a short male confederate (C). In a similar manner, 91 additional male and female adults could violate the personal space of either a tall or a short female C. The results showed that the commuters significantly preferred to intrude into the short, rather than the tall, Cs' spaces. This discrimination occurred for both male and female Cs. Also, female commuters invaded the space of the short Cs significantly more frequently than did the male commuters.[125]

---

124 Daniel Freeman, Ph.D. and Jason Freeman, "Does Our Height Influence Our Mental Health?" *Psychology Today,* January 30, 2014, https://www.psychologytoday.com/us/blog/know-your-mind/201401/does-our-height-influence-our-mental-health
125 Marc E. Caplan and Morton Goldman, "Personal Space Violations as A Function of Height," *The*

From *Psychology Today:*

> According to Julius Fast, author of the groundbreaking clas-
> sic, "Body Language," (revised in 2002) a person who violates
> personal space sends the signal, "You are a non-person, and
> therefore I can move in on you. You do not matter." Fast
> also wrote at length about the work of psychologist Robert
> Sommers who is given credit for coining the term "personal
> space." Sommers pioneered research in exploring the ways
> people interact in personal spaces and consequently how they
> respond to invasions of space.[126]

We've all had our personal space invaded by others, so we all know
what it's like. How many of you men have used a urinal, only for a
stranger to sidle up next to the urinal you're using when there are
multiple other toilets available?

It doesn't seem like a big deal. After all, the incident is brief, and
chances are it won't happen again for a long time. But imagine feeling
that discomfort every time you find yourself in a crowd.

I'm often seriously anxious because of personal space invasions in
crowded areas. I don't attend many concerts, sporting events, fairs, or
festivals as a result. I even modify the times I go to grocery stores or
malls to avoid peak shopping hours because of the claustrophobic-like
sense I feel when around large groups of people.

For those who can't relate to this feeling, imagine driving in your pas-
senger car on the freeway only to find yourself suddenly surrounded
by semitrucks. That's my everyday reality in crowds.

Journal of Social Psychology, November 4, 1980, https://www.tandfonline.com/doi/abs/10.1080
/00224545.1981.9922746
126 Bakari Akil II Ph.D., "Personal Space – How violating unspoken rules can lead to chaos – at
least for you," *Psychology Today,* April 11, 2010, https://www.psychologytoday.com/us/blog/
communication-central/201004/personal-space-how-violating-unspoken-rules-can-lead-chaos-
least

I do make an exception for beer festivals (the alcohol helps dampen the anxiety). Every time I attend one, or find myself in a crowded area, I observe how many times people cut through a line where either I am or another shorter-than-average person is.

From my informal observations and experiences, a person will cut through a line where a shorter person stands about 90 percent of the time.

People don't do this consciously and certainly not maliciously. But when it happens all the time, it leads to feeling my personal space is less important than everybody else's, and, as Julius Fast says, that I do not matter.

In the documentary *S&M: Short and Male*, two men, one tall and one short, conducted a street-walking experiment. They walked against foot traffic on a busy sidewalk from point A to point B while wearing a small camera to verify how many times each got bumped into. The taller man faced little resistance, as people moved out of the way for him, showing him respect, and he made it to point B unscathed. The shorter man got bumped into over a dozen times, all the while having to weave through traffic like it was a game of Frogger.

Crowded areas can be stressful, man.

And imagine all that stress with the knowledge you're basically invisible to the people invading your space. They often don't see you nor acknowledge your existence, even when they do run into you.

It's a nasty form of social isolation in the middle of a sea of humanity.

If there were only a way to become taller ...

But becoming taller isn't achievable without great pain, cost, or interruption to life.

We can do things to *look* taller, such as wearing lifts, or wearing properly fitted clothes, which can be difficult to find. We can work on having more confidence or losing the slouch. These things don't change one's height, but they can change the way others perceive us.

To become physically taller, we have two options.

Option one: growth hormones.

There has been a debate for many years on the use of growth hormones for short stature. Take this 2003 article from ABC News:

> When it comes to your child, how short is too short?
>
> That question has experts split in a fierce debate over the safety and ethics and cosmetically enhancing kids' height, following a government advisory panel's recommendation that growth hormone be approved for use in healthy but unusually short children.
>
> The hormone known as Humatrope, made by Eli Lilly, is now approved only for use in children with rare medical conditions. But the Food and Drug Administration is now mulling the possibility of expanding its use to make extremely short children – boys under 5 foot 3 inches and girls under 4 foot 11 inches – grow taller than they naturally would. The cutoff point to be considered eligible for treatment is under age 14.
>
> Some believe approval of human growth hormone for non-medical reasons will rescue "vertically challenged" children from the societal stigma of being small. But others worry about the implications of such a decision: Will this send a message that short stature is a sickness, an abnormality in need of a "cure"?

The cost of growth hormone injections is about $30,000; some report it can cost up to $52,000 per inch.[127] They are painful, as they

---

127 Olga Oksman, "Should Short Kids Take Growth Hormones?" *Tonic,* March 27, 2017, https://

consist of six invasive injections per week for several years. The average child grows about two extra inches as a result.

The article continues:

> But while some believe growth hormones can relieve children of being teased or picked on, many worry giving short but healthy children growth hormones will only further perpetuate the stigma attached to small stature.
>
> "The message we send to society is that any boy who is less than 5-foot-3 is ill and can avail themselves of a remedy. This is very dangerous as it causes people to make judgments of acceptability and normalcy rather than simply being open to variety and variation," explains John Tuohey, directory of Providence Center for Health Care Ethics in Providence, Ore.
>
> "If shortness is medicalized today, what's next?" asks Dr. Jeffrey Bishop, associate professor of internal medicine at the University of Texas Southwestern Medical Center in Dallas.
>
> Like Bishop, Dr. Mark Groshek, of the department of pediatrics at Kaiser Permanente in Centennial, Colo., worries once the door is open for "healing" short people, "we will face increasing pressure to fix or change more and more things that are simply human characteristics and not illnesses." [128]

Parents in the documentary "Short and Male" were conflicted about whether they should allow their children to take growth hormones. They understand the stigma short people live with. Even though the

---

tonic.vice.com/en_us/article/vvkyyy/should-short-kids-take-growth-hormones

128 Jamie Cohen, "Should Short Kids Use Growth Hormones?" *ABC News,* https://abcnews. go.com/Health/story?id=116731&page=1

hormones could cause cancer[129] or an increased chance of a stroke[130] later in life, it was a chance they were all willing to take.

Tanya Osensky, in her fabulous book *Shortchanged: Height Discrimination and Strategies for Social Change*, wrote this:

> With encouragement from pharmaceutical companies, in July 2003 the FDA approved the use of hGH for treatment of children with idiopathic short stature despite the extremely modest effectiveness of treatment – increasing height by one and one-half inches after four years of treatment, estimated to be more than what the person would have obtained without treatment. (As we explore later, such estimates are not based on very scientific measurement or predictions, and there is no way to know with any certainty that the same growth would not have occurred naturally.)
>
> The FDA approval of hGH treatment was pushed by the pharmaceutical companies based on the assumption that short people suffer from psychological and social issues as a result of their stature. However, the studies presented to the FDA proved only that the treatment achieved added one and one-half inches over the predicted height – none of the results of the study even attempted to show an effort on psychological and social well-being of the subjects. Despite discussion about the lack of impact on the subject's psychosocial adjustment, the FDA was persuaded to approve treatment of healthy children without a medical condition.
>
> Since FDA approval was obtained in 2003, thousands of healthy children have been subjected to hGH treatment. By prescribing

---

129 Shirley S. Wang, "Scientists Warn of Risks From Growth Hormone," *The Wall Street Journal*, March 24, 2014, https://www.wsj.com/articles/scientists-warn-of-risks-from-growth-hormone-1395701375

130 "Growth Hormone Treatment Tied To Increased Risk Of Stroke," *American Academy of Neurology*, August 13, 2014, https://www.aan.com/PressRoom/Home/PressRelease/1301

hGH for healthy short children in an attempt to make them taller, doctors in effect are medicating healthy individuals to counteract social prejudice, rather than as a response to a medical disorder. The proliferation of hGH treatment for children without diagnosable growth disorder shows that we as a society believe it is so bad to be short that we need to medically treat short stature even when it is not due to a real medical cause. While there are no data available that identify the exact proportion of children receiving hGH treatment who do or do not have a deficiency, a 2003 report suggests that about 40 percent of children on hGH therapy have no growth hormone deficiency ... On July 23, 2014, the Partnership for Drug-Free Kids released a report on a study of 3,705 students stating that the use of hGH by teens had more than doubled in the previous year, with the number of high school teens in the study who used the therapy increasing from 5 percent in 2012 to 11 percent in 2013.[131]

Well, it's too late for me for get growth hormones. Maybe option two could work out.

Except option two is limb-lengthening surgery.

If you don't know what this is, enjoy the description from Paley Orthopedic and Spine Institute:

Limb lengthening works through a process called distraction osteogenesis. The bone to be lengthened (femur or tibia) is broken during surgery into two segments. The segments are slowly pulled apart, at a rate of one millimeter per day. For stature patients, the lengthening is performed by an intramedullary nail (the precice) that is inserted into the marrow cavity. The new bone will form in the gap, resulting in increased length. Any

---

131   Tanya Osensky, *Shortchanged: Height Discrimination and Strategies for Social Change.* Lebanon, NH: University Press of New England, 2017.

faster and the bone may fail to form in the gap, muscles will become contracted, and nerves may become paralyzed; any slower and the bone will reform the gap, a process known as premature consolidation, which halts the lengthening.[132]

Want a visual? Just go to the link in this footnote.[133]

It hurts. A lot. It can cost between $25,000 and $175,000 to complete, and a patient's recovery could be upward of two years, although nine months is the stated recovery time.

In countries like China, limb lengthening is becoming more popular as they're placing an ever-increasing value to height.

Have fun with that, guys.

Who thinks conversion therapy is a good idea? If you're not familiar with it, conversion therapy tries to change a person's sexual orientation from gay to straight.

All credible medical and mental health professionals have rejected conversion therapy. It's unnecessary and harmful to individuals, and an increasing number of states are rightfully banning the practice.[134]

There's nothing wrong with you if you're born gay or destined to be short; there's nothing about you that needs to be fixed. Yet conversion therapy is frowned upon and remains a fringe practice, whereas growth hormone therapy and limb-lengthening surgery are growing in popularity.

Nobody wants to be short. Parents don't want short children. Sperm banks don't accept our donations. Women don't want to date us.

---

132 "What is Stature Lengthening?" *Paley Orthopedic & Spine Institute,* https://paleyinstitute.org/centers-of-excellence/stature-lengthening/what-is-stature-lengthening/
133 "Cosmetic Limb Lengthening Surgery," Published on January 2, 2016, Video, 3:14, https://www.youtube.com/watch?v=SeL2aTB62Jc
134 Susan Miller, "'Being LGBTQ is not an illness': Record number of states banning conversion therapy," *USA Today,* April 17, 2018, https://www.usatoday.com/story/news/nation/2018/04/17/states-banning-conversion-therapy/518972002/

It's as if society is trying to rid itself of these short undesirables. But we wouldn't be leaning in that direction, right?

Doctors are worried about a slippery slope when it comes to "healing" short people, and parents are aware of the stigma of growing up small and the psychological issues short men face throughout their lives. What's stopping them from terminating a pregnancy if they find out their child will be short?

Since prenatal screening tests were introduced in Iceland in the early 2000s, close to 100 percent of women have opted to terminate their pregnancies if their child tested positive for Down syndrome.[135]

Societies such as China and India practice female infanticide. Societies that practice female infanticide always show signs of bias against females. Among the concerns is the earning power of females versus males, which, as we've established, is a concern for shorter men as well.[136]

As we're learning more about DNA, scientists say parents could have choices in what characteristics they want their children to have.

Antonio Regalado wrote this for *MIT Technology Review*:

> IVF clinics already test the DNA of embryos to spot rare diseases, like cystic fibrosis, caused by defects in a single gene. But the "preimplantation" tests are poised for a dramatic leap forward as it becomes possible to peer more deeply at an embryo's genome and create broad statistical forecasts about the person it would become.
>
> The advance is occurring, say scientists, thanks to a growing flood of genetic data collected from large population studies.

135 Julian Quinones and Arijeta Lajka, "'What kind of society do you want to live in?': Inside the country where Down syndrome is disappearing," *CBS News,* August 14, 2017, https://www.cbsnews.com/news/down-syndrome-iceland/
136 "Ethics Guide – Female infanticide," BBC, http://www.bbc.co.uk/ethics/abortion/medical/infanticide_1.shtml

As statistical models known as predictors gobble up DNA and health information about hundreds of thousands of people, they're getting more accurate at spotting the genetic patterns that foreshadow disease risk. But they have a controversial side, since the same techniques can be used to project the eventual height, weight, skin tone, and even intelligence of an IVF embryo ...

[Company] Genomic Prediction says it will only report diseases – that is, identify those embryos it thinks would develop into people with serious medical problems. Even so, on his blog and in public statements, [researcher] Hsu has for years been developing a vision that goes far beyond that ...

Armed with the U.K. data, Hsu and [Laurent] Tellier claimed a breakthrough. For one easily measured trait, height, they used machine-learning techniques to create a predictor that behaved flawlessly. They reported that the model could, for the most part, predict people's height from their DNA data to within three or four centimeters...

In the case of height, Genomic Prediction hopes to use the model to help identify embryos that would grow into adults shorter than 4'10", the medical definition of dwarfism, says Tellier. There are many physical and psychological disadvantages to being so short. Eventually the company could also have the ability to identify intellectual problems, such as embryos with a predicted IQ of less than 70.[137]

If you think Genomic Prediction, or any other company that will eventually have this ability, will only ever give potential parents information

---

137 Antonio Regalado, "Eugenics 2.0: We're at the Dawn of Choosing Embryos by Health, Height, and More," *Technology Review,* November 1, 2017, https://www.technologyreview. com/s/609204/eugenics-20-were-at-the-dawn-of-choosing-embryos-by-health-height-and- more/

about diseases, you probably think the earth is flat.[138] Remember, healthy kids are now receiving hGH to "correct" a problem that doesn't need correcting.

Nathan Treff, an in vitro fertilization (IVF) specialist who has Type I diabetes, was highlighted in the article mentioned above. His grandfather lost a leg to diabetes, and Treff hopes his three young children don't develop it later. He points out to his partners that had his parents had the DNA test, they would have aborted the pregnancy.

Some states are enacting abortion laws. Indiana's abortion law prohibits abortions because of "race, color, national origin, ancestry, sex, or diagnosis or potential diagnosis of the fetus having Down syndrome or any other disability."[139]

It's nearly impossible to determine the reason for an abortion, as a woman doesn't have to disclose a motive, so it's not clear how the law will work in practice. But one thing is clear: short-statured fetuses do not have equal protection under this law, just as short people don't have protection under antidiscrimination laws in America.

All I can say is my life is worth living, and I'm thankful I was given the chance to live it out.

Now let's do the hard work to get rid of negative stigmas so life is worth living for everyone, instead of taking the easy way out and killing off the undesirables.

---

138 I have no proof of that claim. However, I am calling you an idiot if you believe them.
139 Emma Green, "Should Women Be Able to Abort a Fetus Just Because It's Female," *The Atlantic*, May 16, 2016, https://www.theatlantic.com/politics/archive/2016/05/sex-disability-race-selective-abortion-indiana/482856/

CHAPTER 7:

Eat Shit and Die, Buzzfeed

25 Places You Need To Poop In Before You Die
— Dave and Matt Stopera, Buzzfeed, February 25, 2016[140]

14 Places You Have To Poop At Before You Die
— Spencer Althouse, Buzzfeed, June 18, 2013[141]

#Buzzfeedcaneatshitanddie
— Leslie Bingham

I was going to write a chapter on the benefits of being a short man. I waxed poetic about how some studies show we live longer and/or have a lower risk of cancer,[142] as well as how we make better husbands and life partners.[143]

---

140 Dave and Matt Stopera, "25 Places You Need To Poop In Before You Die," *Buzzfeed,* February 25, 2016, https://www.buzzfeed.com/daves4/i-want-to-poop-there
141 Spencer Althouse, "14 Places You Have To Poop At Before You Die," *Buzzfeed,* June 18, 2013, https://www.buzzfeed.com/spenceralthouse/places-you-have-to-poop-at-before-you-die
142 Carla Herreria, "Short? You Just Might Live Longer," *Huffpost,* Updated December 6, 2017, https://www.huffpost.com/entry/short-men-live-longer-study_n_5299557
143 "A Point of View: Why short men make better husbands," *BBC,* October 5, 2014, https://www.bbc.com/news/magazine-29464446

And then I thought, how many books about racism, sexism, or homophobia would espouse the benefits of being black, female, or gay? They might exist, but it defeats the purpose of bringing up an ugly issue. There's no reason to sugarcoat real discrimination.

Instead, I'll highlight my one-sided feud with Buzzfeed, a brainless organization I've despised ever since I saw the heightist video mentioned in chapter 4. My hatred only amplified when I read Pedro Fequiere's article where he says he chooses to remain a victim because he believes everybody else in society should change, but he shouldn't have to.[144]

During my research for the doomed chapter, I came across yet another "article" from Buzzfeed titled "19 Reasons Why Being Short Is The Best."[145] It reinforced the fact that Buzzfeed should eat shit and die.

Please note, it took two people to put this list together. Two of them. Their names are Leonora Epstein and Kristin Chirico.

These two adults are such dumbshits that they put together a list that a single elementary school student of lower-than-average intelligence could whip out in under twenty minutes.

According to this powerhouse dream team of shit-eaters, a great reason to be short is "Even though reaching things may be an issue, tall people always seem to be friendly to help a stranger out."

Relying on others to do menial tasks for you is not a good thing.

They continue, "You can always hem pants shorter...but you can't make too-short pants longer. So, you win."

Win what? Yeah, that's right, nothing. This is a universal truth for everyone, just as dressing up will get you greater respect from others.

144 #Buzzfeedcaneatshitanddie
145 Leonora Epstein and Kristin Chirico, "19 Reasons Why Being Short Is The Best," *Buzzfeed,* October 28, 2013, https://www.buzzfeed.com/leonoraepstein/reasons-why-being-short-is-the-best

There is nothing short-specific about this. Besides, if you don't know how to hem pants, you must pay someone else to do it. That's not a win; that's a tax for being short.

The brain trust wasn't done: "You can be an expert couchsurfer because you'll always fit on a sofa."

For fuck's sake. They think it's great to be short so you can live a life of discomfort and poverty on stranger's food and semen-stained sofas.

Four of the things on the list had to do with fitting into smaller spaces. Two of them dealt with clothes shopping in multiple departments. Two of the reasons had to do with "worrying" about being tall.

These mental juggernauts – *working together*, mind you – couldn't even come up with nineteen unique reasons why being short is mildly okay, let alone their claim that being short is "the best."

These are not intelligent people. Buzzfeed is littered with this sort of talentless hackery. And the scary thing is they're influencers, which means the people Buzzfeed influences are even less intelligent than the Buzzfeed staff, which should worry all of us.

As of the writing of this book, they get 9 billion content views per month.[146] More than half of those views are accidental clicks, and another couple billion must be people curious about the train wreck of content posted.[147]

However, if someone uses Buzzfeed as a *serious* source of anything – as Big Erica Morin did for her Tedx Talk as highlighted in chapter 3 – it makes it easy to spot someone you shouldn't take seriously, so Buzzfeed does help weed out intellectual lightweights.

---

146 "Advertise With Buzzfeed," https://advertise.buzzfeed.com/
147 I base these assumptions on the hope that so many people worldwide couldn't possibly be so dumb as to enjoy lists that were obviously thrown together by people who are on their potty break, dreaming of pooping in one of the exotic locations you just have to poop in or at before you die.

Hey, please don't think I'm a raging sexist and only ripping on stupid women. Buzzfeed is plagued by stupid men, too. Take a gander at the literal shitshow the Stopera brothers and Spencer Althouse produce:

"25 Places You Need To Poop In Before You Die"? No, Buzzfeed, the only place I poop in is the toilet.

"14 Places You Have To Poop At Before You Die"? Again, no, Buzzfeed, why would I poop at anything?

What sort of physical gymnastics do I have to engage in to poop *at* something? Am I standing on my hands and aiming my bare bunghole at my friends' television because they are watching *The Big Bang Theory*, possibly the unfunniest sitcom ever created,[148] and I want to give them a tangible review of their taste in entertainment?[149]

If you hadn't noticed, the words *in* and *at* in the titles are wholly unnecessary, just like Buzzfeed as an organization is wholly unnecessary.

Buzzfeed is like the junk food aisle in a grocery store, except it's full of the worst and least desirable of junk foods. It's chock-full of crappy candies like Smarties (ironically, as they're mostly morons), Nerds (sorry to the real nerds out there; you're much cooler than anyone who works there), and the vomit and rotten-egg flavors of Jelly Belly candy.

They are uncooked pasta, which is the most useless food in the universe.

It's trendy now to boycott organizations you disagree with for political purposes. People on the left boycotted Chick-fil-A because the CEO said he preferred the traditional definition of marriage, and they also tried to boycott In-N-Out Burger because it donated money to

---

148 "Serious Big Bang Theory – No Laugh Track – S08 Part 1 – Sheldon Gets Robbed," Published August 23, 2015, Video, 3:35, https://www.youtube.com/watch?v=OjthQKzX88g
149 Seriously, try watching *The Big Bang Theory* without the laugh track. It's cringeworthy. I triple-dog dare you.

a Republican.[150] The right recently boycotted Nike because it made Colin Kaepernick, who sparked controversy for not standing for the national anthem before NFL games, the face of its "Just Do It" campaign.[151]

You folks do what you want. At least Chick-fil-A, In-N-Out Burger, and Nike produce amazing products. I'm boycotting Buzzfeed because its content is objectively awful. It's becoming a parody of itself. Today's Buzzfeed headlines[152] include "Hailey Baldwin Accidentally Revealed That Justin Bieber Doesn't Think Kendall Jenner Is Cool" and "What Kind Of Chocolate Are You Based On Your Fave Halloween Candies?"

No thinking person gives a shit about these things. Zero. Hailey Baldwin and Justin Bieber don't care about what's written about them on Buzzfeed.[153] And you don't care what kind of chocolate you are based on your fave Halloween candies.[154]

Hey, Buzzfeed, how about you take all the shit from your pooping articles and eat it. And then die.

Join me in making #Buzzfeedcaneatshitanddie go viral.

Together, we can make a real, positive difference in this world.

---

150 William Sullivan, "Double-Double Failure for the Left's Fast Food Boycotts," *American Thinker,* September 2, 2018, https://www.americanthinker.com/articles/2018/09/doubledouble_failure_for_the_lefts_fast_food_boycotts.html

151 Amy B. Wang and Rachel Siegel, "Trump: Nike 'getting absolutely killed' with boycotts over Colin Kaepernick's 'Just Do It' campaign," *The Washington Post,* September 5, 2018, https://www.washingtonpost.com/business/2018/09/04/people-are-destroying-their-nike-gear-protest-colin-kaepernicks-just-do-it-campaign/?utm_term=.2b64eede0019

152 Today is October 16, 2018. You can hit up Buzzfeed's homepage any day and get content as stupid as what I saw today.

153 Just ask them.

154 There's no way in hell you care about this.

CHAPTER 8:

Identity Politics

*Hold yourself responsible for a higher standard than
anybody expects of you. Never excuse yourself.*
– Henry Ward Beecher

*We need a new diversity – not one based on biological characteristics
and identity politics but a diversity of opinion and worldviews.*
– Ayaan Hirsi Ali

*You take your life in your own hands, and what
happens? A terrible thing: no one to blame.*
– Erica Jong

*The only "ism" I ever want to come out of your mouth is a syllogism.
If I catch you using an "ism" or its analogous "ist" – racist, classist, etc.
– then you will not be permitted to continue speaking until you have
first identified which "ism" you are guilty of at that very moment. You
are not allowed to fault others for being biased or privileged until you
have first identified and examined your own biases and privileges.*
– Adam J. MacLeod, associate law professor, Faulkner University[155]

155   Adam J MacLeod, "Undoing the Dis-Education of Millennials," *New Boston Post,* November 9,
      2017, https://newbostonpost.com/2017/11/09/undoing-the-dis-education-of-millennials/

M&Ms ran a commercial during Super Bowl 52 featuring Gabourey Sidibe. In it, she turns from a brown M&M into a human. At the end, she admires herself in the reflection of a store window and says, "Man, I look good." Her M&M pal retorts, "You're still brown and obese."

The tagline sparked online Twitter riots. People demanded an apology and the firing of everybody involved with the production. #BoycottMM went viral. The football game, one of the most entertaining in recent memory, was a mere side note in the days following, much like after the Janet Jackson/Justin Timberlake "Nipplegate" halftime show from Super Bowl 38, as news outlets spent hours on end spouting the shamefulness of the blatant racism, sexism, and body shaming of a precious ...

Wait, what? That's not what happened?

Oh, sorry!

The commercial featured Danny DeVito turning from a red M&M into a human. Afterward he says, "Man, I look good," and the candy friend said, "You're still short and bald."

And America rejoiced.

Why are some physical characteristics okay to make fun of, but others aren't? Why is it so cringeworthy to think about making fun of Sidibe when it's encouraged to make fun of DeVito?

We're conditioned to treat some groups differently.

It's a simple double standard, identity politics, and the fact that people aren't interested in equality but in special treatment.

Like it or not, identity politics perpetuates the notion that some groups are inherently superior to others. Let's allow Evergreen State College President George Bridges explain in an op-ed he wrote for the *Seattle Times*:

At The Evergreen State College, where I serve as president, 90 percent of our students belong to at least one group traditionally underserved by higher education: first-generation college students, low income, people of color, veterans, people with disabilities or students of nontraditional age. These students face personal challenges that many in previous generations didn't. Many are reluctant to engage faculty and staff with questions or arguments out of fear of failure or rejection. They and their families have no experience in navigating college studies, debating academic issues and ideas or pursuing critical sources of financial aid.

Providing safe spaces for these students – that is, places and contexts in which they can reflect on and address these unfamiliar issues without fear of failure or rejection by others – proves critical to their success. As colleges and universities seek to increase rates of student retention and graduation, we must (and we are) creating these spaces.[156]

These are issues every incoming freshman faces, regardless of sex, race, income bracket, or if others in their family attended college before them. To believe that only underserved groups face these challenges is ludicrous.

College is the place to get familiar with all of this stuff.

Let's take his examples one by one.

"Many are reluctant to engage faculty or staff with questions or arguments out of fear of failure or rejection." When dealing with individual faculty or staff members you are unfamiliar with, yes, some will be fearful of failure or rejection. Most students will be nervous at one

156 George S. Bridges, "Why students need trigger warnings and safe places," *The Seattle Times,* August 29, 2016, https://www.seattletimes.com/opinion/why-students-need-trigger-warnings-and-safe-places/

time or another with these fears. This is not a special hurdle for underserved students.

"They and their families have no experience in navigating college studies ..." An individual with only a high school education or GED most certainly does not have experience navigating college studies. It would be odd if they did. All individuals going to college for the first time will have to figure this out. In my experience, it came down to waking up in time for class, going to class, doing the homework, and taking the tests. That's how one "navigates" college studies. It's the same way you navigate high school studies. This is not a special hurdle to underserved students.

"Debating academic issues and ideas ..." College is where an individual gets to debate academic issues and ideas. That's part of the appeal of attending college. High school is not a hotbed of intellectual debate, so having a vast amount of experience debating academic issues and ideas would be very unusual for an incoming freshman to any college. This is not a special hurdle to underserved students.

"Or pursuing critical sources of financial aid." Most people aren't lucky enough to have Mom and Dad write a check for their college tuition. That's why all colleges and universities have financial aid departments that help students with this. The Evergreen State College is no exception.[157] Again, this is not a special hurdle to underserved students.

These are the explicit examples Bridges uses in his argument for providing safe spaces to minority students, yet none of these examples seem to affect any one group over another.

Every single thing Bridges listed was true for me. I was nervous and reluctant with faculty and staff, had no experience navigating college studies, had no experience whatsoever debating academic issues, and had no idea what I was doing when it came to financial aid. And to

157 https://www.evergreen.edu/financialaid

think that I would have needed a safe space to deal with these issues is insulting.

I find it hard to believe a college president would think so lowly of his students. My only takeaway is that he thinks the underserved students are inferior to other groups of students, and as a result, they need coddling.

It's the soft bigotry of low expectations, alive and well in our institutions of higher education. President Bridges is a bigot and doesn't even know it.

If you expect less from some groups based on a perception of "underserved" status, you are a bigot. On the flip side, if you expect more from certain groups based on a perception of "privileged" status, you are a bigot. If you expect less from one group, you innately expect more from others.

That, folks, is bigotry. Expecting less from a black person just because of the color of his or her skin is racist. Expecting more from a white person based on the color of his or her skin is racist.

Instead of treating students as individuals and giving them the benefit of the doubt, Bridges preemptively clumps them into groups expecting fiery meltdowns over navigating college studies and assumes they need a safe space as a result.

He assumes their fragility based on the tribe he's put them in.

When you treat adults like children, they act like children.

See chapter 2 for evidence of their childish behavior. Yes, Bridges is the president of the same Evergreen College where students had epic temper tantrums when a professor thought forcing white people off campus for the day was a bad idea.

Treating people differently based on their oppressed group status is not a way to achieve equality. It's a way to pump out generations of students who feel they deserve special treatment based on the tribe with whom they identify.

The videos from the Evergreen College student takeover show mobs of entitled turdlets acting out because they weren't getting their way. When others didn't comply with their demands, they lashed out in furious anger.[158]

During the fiasco, Bridges wasn't allowed to use simple hand gestures while speaking because students said they were signs of aggression, or microaggressions.

He also wasn't allowed to use the restroom without an escort because they didn't want him to escape.[159]

He helped create the environment, so I guess he has nobody to blame but himself, which he probably will because blaming the kids for their own actions might be construed as racist.

Nice work grooming the future of America, dude.

When you treat people differently, you give them a different set of rules to live by. That's fine if we're dealing with children or those with mental disabilities. But to do so with fully functioning adults is not a way to achieve equality. And when they don't receive that special treatment in other parts of their life, they feel as if they are being discriminated against, which is exactly what these minority groups claim to be fighting against.

Catch-22 much?

I'm going to reference the microaggression example I used in chapter 2 as an example. As a refresher, here is a black woman's example from microaggressions.com:

158 "Student takeover of Evergreen State College," Published on May 27, 2017, Video, 7:14, https://www.youtube.com/watch?v=bO1agIlLlhg&t=10s

159 Jason Rantz, "Student activists sent Evergreen president to psychologist," *770 KTTH,* October 31, 2017, http://mynorthwest.com/799775/evergreen-president-psychologist/?

The offending statement: "Look, it's a dog walker, you have such a cool job!" (said) A white woman in the lobby of my condo. To which I replied, "These are my dogs and I live here." Her [totally oblivious] "Oh! He does too!" I shook my head and got into the elevator. It felt as if she were implying that a (*sic*) Afro-American person – much less a woman — could (*sic*) afford to live in this building.

The white woman treated both her and the man the same way, yet she is still convinced the white woman's actions/words toward her were bigoted.

Remember the Serena Williams meltdown at the US Open that I also mentioned in chapter 2? She said, "I'm here fighting for women's rights and women's equality and all kinds of stuff." In the aftermath of her defeat, *Herald Sun* cartoonist Mark Knight drew an overexaggerated caricature of Williams throwing her tantrum, which, if you look at his other cartoons, is his style of cartooning. As if on cue, the outrage mob called the cartoon sexist and racist, and Knight suspended his Twitter account because of abuse toward his family.[160]

The *Herald Sun* defended Knight and used the front page of the paper to highlight other caricatures of famous people. As is the norm with his caricatures, physical features are always exaggerated.[161] If you're fat, you will be portrayed as fatter. If you have big ears, your ears will be portrayed as bigger. If you're short, you will be portrayed as shorter, as seen with the Donald Trump/Vladimir Putin cartoon near the end of this link.[162]

---

160 "Herald Sun backs Mark Knight's cartoon on Serena Williams," *Herald Sun,* September 11, 2018, https://www.heraldsun.com.au/news/victoria/herald-sun-backs-mark-knights-cartoon-on-serena-williams/news-story/30c877e3937a510d64609d89ac521d9f

161 Adam Taylor, "Aussie newspaper doubles down on Serena cartoon decried as racist, puts it on the front page," *Washington Post,* September 12, 2018, https://www.washingtonpost.com/world/2018/09/12/aussie-newspaper-doubles-down-serena-cartoon-called-racist-puts-it-front-page/?utm_term=.78df8afc6576

162 "Herald Sun backs Mark Knight's Serena Cartoon," *News Mail,* September 11, 2018, https://www.news-mail.com.au/news/herald-sun-backs-mark-knights-cartoon-on-serena-wi/3517987/

Should I be upset with Knight for portraying Putin as shorter than his listed five foot seven and call him a heightist and tweet angry things at him?

Of course not, that's ridiculous.

Williams, fighting for "equality and all kinds of stuff," was treated just as any famous person is treated when he or she is deserving of such a cartoon. And when Williams is treated equally, which is what she claims to be fighting for, it's deemed sexist and racist.

Please don't forget that Williams is a very wealthy athlete with entitlement issues, and she's the adult version of the child bully nobody should like. In the past she's called a female umpire "unattractive inside" and "a loser." During the latest tantrum, she repeatedly demanded an apology and told the male umpire he would never work another one of her matches.

Makes you wonder who is actually unattractive inside.

Williams, and any other entitled bully, doesn't want equality. She wants things to go her way.

People don't really want equality, even if those are the words that come out of their mouths. They want special consideration based on the genitals they possess or the amount of melanin in their skin.

Equality doesn't happen by virtue signaling. Equality happens when we start treating people as our equals. Crying sexism and racism when you are finally treated like everyone else is stifling societal progress, and it's helping further divide us as a country.

While doing research on the wage gap, I came across this gem from entrepreneur.com:

> The reality is, there's a gender pay gap between self-employed men and women, too. According to a study by cloud accounting company Freshbooks, it's even larger than the overall pay

gap: Self-employed women make 28 percent less than self-employed men, or 72 cents for every dollar a male earns.

That's despite the fact that 33 percent of traditionally employed women surveyed by Freshbooks said they'll leave their office job by 2020 to earn more money, and 70 percent of self-employed women report they make as much or more money as they did when they were traditionally employed. However, Freshbooks also learned that 20 percent of self-employed females say they have to charge less than their male counterparts to attract and retain clients.[163]

The article claims self-employed women are discriminated against because they have to charge less than their male counterparts to attract and retain clients. This is not a gender-specific issue. Every self-employed individual, male or female, must compete against each other to attract and retain clients. That's how you survive in business.

To try to make this a gender-specific issue is nonsensical. This is a case where women are treated as equals, yet they feel as if they are being discriminated against. This rhetoric doesn't help women, and it may discourage some women from even trying to become an entrepreneur, which is the opposite of what I think the point of the article is.

Don't believe me? How nonsensical is the sentence "Freshbooks also learned that 20 percent of self-employed short men say they have to charge less than their taller male counterparts to attract and retain clients." More than likely you'd roll your eyes, tell them to get over it, and adapt because being an entrepreneur isn't an easy competition.

You must allow yourself to play by the same rules and live with the same consequences as everybody else and not expect special treatment. If not, we'll never achieve the type of equality where your race,

163   Lydia Belanger, "How to Fight the Gender Pay Gap as a Self-Employed Woman – and Maximize Your Income," *Entrepreneur,* September 4, 2018, https://www.entrepreneur.com/article/319265

sex, sexual orientation, or height doesn't matter, which is what we should all be striving for.

American lawyer Amy Chua wrote:

> When groups feel threatened, they retreat into tribalism. When groups feel mistreated and disrespected, they close ranks and become more insular, more defensive, more punitive, more us-versus-them.

> In America today, every group feels this way to some extent. Whites and blacks, Latinos and Asians, men and women, Christians, Jews, and Muslims, straight people and gay people, liberals and conservatives – all feel their groups are being attacked, bullied, persecuted, discriminated against.

> Of course, one group's claims to feeling threatened and voiceless are often met by another group's derision because it discounts their own feelings of persecution – but such is political tribalism...

> For the Left, identity politics has long been a means to "confront rather than obscure the uglier aspects of American history and society."

> But in recent years, whether because of growing strength or growing frustration with the lack of progress, the Left has upped the ante. A shift in tone, rhetoric, and logic has moved identity politics away from inclusion – which had always been the Left's watchword – toward exclusion and division. As a result, many on the Left have turned against universalist rhetoric (for example, All Lives Matter), viewing it as an attempt to erase the specificity of the experience and oppression of historically marginalized minorities.

The new exclusivity is partly epistemological, claiming that out-group members cannot share in the knowledge possessed by in-group members ("You can't understand X because you are white"; "You can't understand Y because you're not a woman"; "You can't speak about Z because you're not queer"). The idea of "cultural appropriation" insists, among other things, "These are our group's symbols, traditions, patrimony, and out-group members have no right to them."

For much of the Left today, anyone who speaks in favor of group blindness is on the other side, indifferent to or even guilty of oppression. For some, especially on college campuses, anyone who doesn't swallow the anti-oppression orthodoxy hook, line and sinker – anyone who doesn't acknowledge "white supremacy" in America – is a racist …

Once identity politics gains momentum, it inevitably subdivides, giving rise to ever-proliferating group identities demanding recognition.[164]

Louis Sarkozy, a contributor to the *Washington Examiner* website's *Beltway Confidential* blog, a student in philosophy and religion at New York University, and the youngest son of former French President Nicolas Sarkozy, wrote:

Intellectual individuality, the basis for rational discourse between thinking human beings, is being discarded in favor of groupthink. No longer are students espousing their opinions or views based on moral and rational reasoning, but are instead robotically adopting the opinions shared by members of their specific race, ethnicity, religion, or political party.

---

164 Amy Chua, "How America's identity politics went from inclusion to division," *The Guardian,* March 1, 2018, https://www.theguardian.com/society/2018/mar/01/how-americas-identity-politics-went-from-inclusion-to-division

When it comes to college political correctness, this has reached tragicomical proportions, where the validity of an argument on any topic is no longer evaluated on its evidence or logic, but instead on the identity of the individual making the argument. On college campuses people are regularly disqualified from a political conversation on, say, police brutality, if they are not black, or Hispanic, or a member of a "persecuted" minority group, since they have not experienced the "persecution" themselves.

In these conversations, facts do not matter. Nor do the intellectual conclusions surmised from these facts. Instead, the most salient element is the origin or background of the speaker. In American society there is a "ladder of victimization" that ranks opinions not on merit or truthfulness, but instead on the level of perceived persecution experienced by the holder of the opinion.[165]

The identity politics game is dangerous.

It's dangerous because it's stripping our ability to be objective players in life, and it fosters a victim mentality.

We're losing the ability to take a step back and evaluate our beliefs and actions as an individual. Instead, we're being forced to think like others in our group because if we don't, we will be socially ostracized.

Modern-day identity politics is, as Chua says, an "us-versus-them" endeavor. Either you're with us or against us, and if you're against us, then fuck you.

Dave Rubin, from his YouTube video titled "Identity Politics Must Come to an End" said this:

One of the themes we consistently talk about here at the

---

165 Louis Sarkozy, "Identity politics and the death of the individual," *Washington Examiner,* January 18, 2018, https://www.washingtonexaminer.com/identity-politics-and-the-death-of-the-individual

Rubin Report is why it's important to judge people as individuals and not as a collective. You, as an individual, are much more than your immutable characteristics, be it your skin color, your religion, or your sexuality. To judge you on those characteristics is actually what the essence of prejudice really is. Prejudice, of course, means to pre-judge. So if you look at a black person, or a Muslim person, or a gay person, and think that you know what they think, or more importantly, how they should think, based on those characteristics, then you are actually the one who's being prejudiced. Sadly, many of the people who accuse others of bigotry and racism these days are often the people who practice this brand of prejudice the most without even realizing that they're doing so. Just look at some of the things my friends Larry Elder, Maajid Nawaz, and Ayaan Hirsi Ali are called by the so-called tolerant side.[166]

Rubin knows firsthand how modern-day identity politics plays out. He's gay, married, Jewish, and liberal, but he gets branded a Nazi and "alt-right" by the progressives who dislike him for having guests with different opinions on his YouTube show. He also doesn't buy into the VM or identity politics.

You're a monster if you don't think or act the way others believe you should.

Black conservatives, such as Thomas Sowell, Tommy Sotomayor, Larry Elder, Walter Williams, Condoleezza Rice, Stacey Dash, and Sage Steele, get called "race traitors" and "Uncle Toms" by fellow black people.

Steele, an ESPN anchor, said the following during a discussion on race for the "Under Our Skin" forum held in Tampa, Florida, in February 2017:

---

166   The Rubin Report, "Identity Politics Must Come to an End," Published November 15, 2017, Video, 3:22, https://www.youtube.com/watch?v=JtDYS6w7ArY

There are times that I believe that we, as African Americans, can be hypocritical, and that is to not look ourselves in the mirror when we are saying certain things and blaming other groups for one thing when we are doing the exact same thing …The worst racism that I have received, and I mean thousands and thousands over the years, is from Black people, who in my mind I thought would be the most accepting because there has been that experience. But, even as recent as the last couple of weeks, the words that I have had thrown at me I can't repeat here and it's 99 percent from people with my skin color. But if a white person said those words to me, what would happen? … How do we, as our foundation, address this honestly with each other and these communities? Because to me, if we don't start with ourselves in any issue, how can you point your fingers at somebody else?[167]

If you read The Root article I referenced to get this quote, the author, Stephen A. Crockett Jr., makes both Rubin's and Steele's points for them. Crockett wants Steele to act and think the way he believes she should as a woman of color, and because she doesn't, he is basically socially ostracizing her. He wrote, "Here's to hoping she'll find her way, but my suspicion is that a black woman who will let MMA fighter Chael Sonnen touch her hair (like she's an animal on display) on national television has been permanently banned from the cookout."

Somehow Crockett, and many others, found her statement controversial. Telling the truth about the reality of your personal situation shouldn't be divisive, yet people were upset with her comments because they believed it disparaged black people.

---

167 Stephen A. Crockett Jr., "Sage Steele Keeps Sage Steele-ing; Claims Worst Racism She's Received Is From Blacks," *The Root,* February 22, 2017, https://www.theroot.com/sage-steele-keeps-sage-steele-ing-claims-the-worst-rac-1792610874

Justifiably criticizing racists shouldn't be controversial, regardless of their skin color, but that's the situation we've cultivated and encouraged through identity politics.

Shitty behavior must be called out regardless of the race or gender of the offender.

Those disparaging Steele can't handle her criticizing them. They want her to listen to them and change her ways, but they aren't willing to listen to her valid criticisms of them to change their ways.

We've created a world where people of the same groups aren't allowed to criticize fellow group members lest they be ostracized from their own community. It forces groupthink or, at the very least, a silencing of different opinions.

If you can't take simple criticism from someone in your group, you're not going to be able to handle criticism from someone from the outside. And if you can't handle outside criticism, what makes you think people in different groups will accept the criticisms you're throwing at them?

If you don't want other people to tell you what to do or how to live your life, why would others let you tell them what to do or how to live their lives?

Documentary filmmaker Cassie Jaye, a former feminist, was ostracized by her feminist allies when she made *The Red Pill*, a documentary about the men's rights movement. They boycotted her film and spread inaccuracies about its contents to demonize her for evolving her opinions on gender-related topics.

Jaye tells of her ostracization in her TedxMarin speech, "Meeting the Enemy: A Feminist Comes to Terms with the Men's Rights Movement":

> And I learned a difficult lesson: When you start to humanize your enemy, you, in turn, may be dehumanized by your

community. And that's what happened to me.

Rather than debating the merit of the issues addressed in the film, I became the target of a smear campaign. And people who had never seen the movie protested outside the theater doors just chanting that it was harmful to women. It certainly is not. But I understand their mind-set.

If I never made this movie, and I heard there was a documentary screening about men's rights activists that didn't show them as monsters, I too would have protested the screenings or at least signed the petitions to ban the film because I was told that they were my enemy ...

The greatest challenge I faced was peeling back the layers of my own bias.[168]

Her greatest challenge was being objective about herself.

Those who buy into the identity politics and VM game have a harder time seeing their own biases and being objective about themselves because it's not required of them. They're taught to find fault in others and in those they perceive as their victimizers.

In an interview with author and podcaster Stefan Molyneux, Jaye readily admits what most people embroiled in identity politics and the victim mentality won't:

When I was a feminist, I did have the victimhood mentality that was a chip on my shoulder that I brought this kind of seeing the world through Eeyore's eyes ... the world was stacked against me. And I'm sure I brought that into relationships, I'm sure I brought that into job interviews, and I'm sure I wasn't a great

168 Cassie Jaye, "Meeting The Enemy: A Feminist Comes To Terms With the Men's Rights Movement," Published on October 18, 2017, at TedxMarin, Video, 14:47, https://www.youtube.com/watch?v=3WMuzhQXJoY

person to be around all the time. So I do think that victimhood mentality of feminists is holding them back from really living their best life and having a fulfilling life, whether it's in relationships or their job.

When I was a feminist I definitely wanted to blame, and I didn't necessarily take responsibility or accountability for my own actions and not getting the job or not having that relationship work. *I wanted to blame.* And I left feminism and I do find myself really looking inward and reading self-help books and just trying to figure out how to change the way you look at the world to improve your life rather than making the world change for you.[169]

When playing the victim, you don't have to take responsibility for your actions or for self-improvement, or for holding yourself accountable for the bigotry you hold within yourself toward others. You're the victim, society is the victimizer, and therefore, it must change to appease you and others who look like you. Identity politics is helping stunt the personal growth of generations of people because there's no incentive to be better personally if the problems in society always lie with everyone else.

Those playing the identity politics and VM game aren't holding themselves to the same standards they demand of others.

They demand an end to discrimination of *their* group, they demand *their* acceptance, and they demand society to change for *them*, yet the last things they are willing to do is confront their own biases to end their own discrimination of others, to accept others for who they are or what they believe, or to make personal changes for their own betterment and ultimately for the betterment of society.

---

169   Cassie Jaye and Stefan Molyneux, "Identity Politics," Published on February 26, 2018, Video,
      1:33:13, https://www.youtube.com/watch?v=4csFvhJ2pF8

They are happy if others appease their group because they get what they want. And when they get what they want, they will inevitably want more. Equality is not the objective. Getting more is the objective.

Demanding others to bend to your will is often selfish and shortsighted.

People don't enjoy it when you (more than likely incorrectly) call them sexist, racist, and homophobic, especially when you're showing your ignorance and intolerance while doing so.

Let's revisit what Chua said regarding identity politics: "The new exclusivity is partly epistemological, claiming that out-group members cannot share in the knowledge possessed by in-group members ("You can't understand X because you are white", "You can't understand Y because you're not a woman", "You can't speak about Z because you're not queer")."

This is a shortsighted and oblivious way to view the world because it shuts down any civil discussion before it occurs. This mentality reinforces the idea that some groups are beyond criticism based on their group or victim status.

Sometimes the best knowledge comes from objective, not subjective, sources.

I mean, come on, you don't want to be known as the person who only surrounds yourself with "yes-men," do you? Only getting one-sided information or opinions to reinforce your already existing beliefs? Sure, it feels good, but it's not a good way to stoke social change.

Chances are you know the guy who only surrounds himself with "yes-men," and you probably don't respect him.

The beauty of life is if you come together and hear each other out, you can start to understand, or empathize with, another's life experiences. Shutting out what you feel may be criticism or outside opinions that don't match your own is not only not desirable, but it also can cripple any decent discourse needed to help make the situation better.

Has anyone ever offered you a breath mint? It's because your breath smelled like shit. But you're too close to the situation to realize it, even though the problem is spewing from your mouth an inch below your nose.

Someone was kind enough to let you know the smell of hot garbage isn't a desirable odor coming from a facial orifice. And it's not something to get angry about.

I got angry when taller people told me I needed more confidence.

"Fuck you," I thought. "I have enough confidence,[170] and how could you possibly know? You haven't been this height since middle school. You don't know what I've endured!"

This happened many times, and I couldn't, or refused to, see they were correct. I was too close to my own situation to step back and objectively see what everybody else saw.

Sometimes it's okay to listen to those outside of your group.

Sometimes it's okay to accept the breath mint.

We shouldn't automatically dismiss an outsider's opinion because the person sharing it doesn't look like us or doesn't believe the same things.

Be open-minded. Be objective. Be fair.

That's the only way we'll ever make social progress. It's not shutting out dissenting opinions; it's listening to each other and confronting our own biases when necessary, just as we ask others to do for us.

---

170 I didn't.

Social change is desirable if we go about it the right way. I don't think going about it as fragmented pieces fighting for special privileges is the right way.

Now imagine this:

Thousands of rabid short people take to the streets with blowhorns and meme-worthy signs, such as "Check your height privilege" and "My height doesn't determine my worth." We shut down city streets and make people late for work, doctor's appointments, and interviews. We don't care if your grandpa is dying in the hospital with only minutes left to live and you can't get to him to say goodbye, you will listen to *us*!

We demand social change.

We demand equal pay for equal work.

We demand an end to bullying against short boys.

We demand an end to the anti-short-person media bias.

We demand Hollywood to tell our stories.

We demand to be part of the laws that give protection to other marginalized groups.

We demand equal representation in politics because how can tall people properly legislate from our point of view? They have no idea what we go through daily to merely survive. We want more people in politics that look like *us*!

We demand body positivity campaigns and an end to short shaming.

We demand an end to systemic heightism.

We demand to be believed.

We do this because whose mind isn't changed by a good old-fashioned rally in the downtown of a major metropolis?

We've been silenced for too long! You will hear our voices, and you will show us justice! The justice where we get what we demand!

You know, we'll just do what other marginalized groups do these days: yell at the top of our lungs for social acceptance and change until we get it.

This scenario is my first fucking nightmare.

I would like to see some change but not the kind of change that relies on the social justice warrior fuckery taking place today.

The social justice tactics taking place today are irrational and divisive. It's not about equality any longer; it's about getting more for your group. It's about glorifying the VM and excluding others from the party.

It's counterproductive to real, sustainable social change.

The more we play the identity politics game, the more we'll become divided and insist others can't understand our lived experiences, and therefore, we shouldn't have an opinion on them. The more we shut out other's voices, the less we'll understand them. The less we understand others, the easier it is to demonize them. The easier it is to demonize them, the easier it is to blame them for our shortcomings. The easier it is to blame them for our shortcomings, the easier it is to cultivate the victim mentality and insist that the ones we demonize are our victimizers. The further into the victim mentality we get, the more we want validation from people who have similar life experiences. This leads back to identity politics and glorification of the victim mentality, reassuring us that everybody else must change to right the wrongs thrown upon our group.

You can see how this can snowball into a shitstorm of ridiculousness.

This is what's happening in society.

This is not what I want for my fellow shorties. I think we're better than all that nonsense.

CHAPTER 9:

The Endgame

Did Gandhi take a knee?
— Dan Hawkins

How is this revolution to take place? Nobody knows how it will take place in humanity, but every man feels it clearly in himself. And yet in our world everybody thinks of changing humanity, and nobody thinks of changing himself.
— Leo Tolstoy

If you want to change the way people respond to you, change the way you respond to people.
— Timothy Leary

We but mirror the world. All the tendencies present in the outer world are to be found in the world of our body. If we could change ourselves, the tendencies in the world would also change. As a man changes his own nature, so does the attitude of the world change towards him.
— Mahatma Gandhi

The endgame, of course, is to end unjust discrimination.

The only way that happens is through confronting our own biases and learning to listen to each other.

The most important thing you can do to change the culture is to change your choices and not rely on trying to change others.

Be a maverick, not a political drone of what you think others think you should be.

Besides, chances are you're not going to change anyone's mind.

And I don't expect this book has changed your mind on anything.

You know Ben Shapiro's saying: "Facts don't care about your feelings." Well, Mr. Shapiro, come to find out, feelings don't care about your facts.

Ozan Varol, a rocket scientist turned law professor and author, wrote this:

> If you had asked me this question – How do you change a mind? – two years ago, I would have given you a different answer.
>
> As a former scientist, I would have cautioned you to rely on objective facts and statistics. Develop a strong case for your side, back it up with hard, cold, irrefutable data, and voilà!
>
> Drowning the other person with facts, I assumed, was the best way to prove that global warming is real, the war on drugs has failed, or the current business strategy adopted by your risk-averse boss with zero imagination is not working.
>
> Since then, I've discovered a significant problem with this approach.
>
> It doesn't work.

The mind doesn't follow the facts. Facts, as John Adams put it, are stubborn things, but our minds are even more stubborn. Doubt isn't always resolved in the face of facts for even the most enlightened among us, however credible and convincing those facts might be.

As a result of the well-documented confirmation bias, we tend to undervalue evidence that contradicts our beliefs and over-value evidence that confirms them. We filter out inconvenient truths and arguments on the opposing side. As a result, our opinions solidify, and it becomes increasingly harder to disrupt established patterns of thinking.

If you have any doubts about the power of confirmation bias, think back to the last time you Googled a question. Did you meticulously read each link to get a broad objective picture? Or did you simply skim through the links looking for the page that confirms what you already believed was true? And let's face it, you'll always find that page, especially if you're willing to click through to Page 12 on the Google search results.[171]

Science writer Elizabeth Svoboda wrote:

Most of us have a strong drive to hold on to pre-existing be-liefs and convictions, which keep us anchored in the world. When your stance on controversial issues both cements your group identity and plants you in opposition to perceived en-emies, changing it can exact a high personal toll.

"We are social animals instinctively reliant on our tribe for safety and protection," says risk perception expert David Ropeik, author of How Risky Is It, Really?. "Any disloyalty literally feels dangerous, like the tribe will kick you out. This effect is

---

171 Ozan Varol, "Facts Don't Change People's Minds. Here's What Does," *Heleo*, September 8, 2017, https://heleo.com/facts-dont-change-peoples-minds-heres/16242/

magnified in people already worried."

Defection, in short, feels as terrifying as stepping off a window ledge – and to a certain extent, this fear is justified. When you think and behave in ways that separate you from members of your close community, you're likely to experience at least some level of exclusion.

There's a certain amount of plain old inertia at work, too. Researchers who study how people resolve cognitive dissonance – the uneasy feeling of holding inconsistent beliefs – note that most people would rather deny or downplay new, uncomfortable information than reshape their worldview to accommodate it. From that perspective, it's less surprising that your friend whose behavior toward women is above reproach is more than willing to support politicians who've committed sexual assault ...

When doubts *do* creep in, they can have a paradoxical effect, leading people to dig in their heels even more.[172]

Nowhere is this more apparent than in our current political environment.

People loyal to either major political party always find themselves in a position where they're forced to defend the indefensible.

Let's take the example Svoboda gives us above: sexual assault, which I hope we can all agree is one of the worst things you can do to another human.

---

172 Elizabeth Svoboda, "Why Is It So Hard to Change People's Minds?" *Greater Good Magazine*, June 27, 2017, https://greatergood.berkeley.edu/article/item/why_is_it_so_hard_to_change_peoples_minds

There are often two things at play here. The first is a reluctance to defect from your tribe even if, objectively speaking, your side is in the wrong.

There's no shortage of sexual assault claims against either Republicans or Democrats, yet each side is quick to defend those accused on their side of the political aisle.

For all the hate Trump has received from Democrats for the sexual misconduct claims against him, they have apparently forgotten all the support they gave to Bill Clinton after his marital infidelities and the rape accusations against him.

The list of sexual misconduct allegations against politicians is staggering, yet more times than not people who vote "R" will defend and explain away the misdeeds of Republicans, and people who vote "D" will do the very same for their Democrats.

So, what it is, folks? Political partisanship or human decency? It seems like both sides are lacking in the human decency category.

No matter how anybody tries to justify their support for politicians credibly accused of sexual misconduct, it's a steaming hot pile of hypocrisy on both sides. Besides, sexual assault isn't a political issue, so let's all try to stop making it one.

The second thing at play is people digging in their heels when faced with information that's damaging to their beliefs.

Sticking with the sexual assault theme, let's look at the Brett Kavanaugh Supreme Court hearings of 2018.

If you don't know what happened, Kavanaugh was Trump's pick for a seat on the Supreme Court. Christine Blasey Ford accused Kavanaugh of sexual assault while they were at a house party in the summer of 1982, when Kavanaugh was seventeen years old and Ford was fifteen. Both Ford and Kavanaugh had to testify in front of Congress.

It was easy to predict, yet fascinating to watch, the brouhaha that occurred. Both political sides dug in their heels and talked past each other instead of to each other, and most people seemed unable to use their own reasoning to come to an unbiased, nonpolitical conclusion. Both sides insisted their evidence and logic (and rhetoric) were correct. As the fiasco continued, the Left moved further left in their convictions, and the Right moved further right with theirs. By the end, the Left, which started out being against Kavanaugh, was convinced he was one of the worst candidates with a severely troubling past and couldn't possibly sit on the Supreme Court without controversy. The Right was more convinced than ever that he was the correct man for the job, and all the FBI investigations and high school/college shenanigans proved he had a near angelic history when compared to anyone else.

All these conclusions were based on the same evidence.

So no, I don't expect to change your mind about anything I've presented in this book. But I would like you to take a step back for a few minutes and try to objectively evaluate how you reacted to some of what I wrote earlier.

How did you react to my opinions on the gender wage gap? If you believe the wage gap exists because of discrimination, you probably got angry and skimmed over a lot of what I wrote because those opinions didn't feel good to you. Chances are you didn't bother to read the articles or studies referenced in the footnotes, and, if you did, your goal was probably to discredit them, not learn from them. You may think I'm an uneducated misogynist and a pawn for the alt-right, spouting off about things I couldn't possibly understand because I'm a white male. And as a white male, I have a white male privilege that I should check before coming to conclusions that don't affect me.

Yet, how did you react when you learned short men also face a similar, if not more severe, wage gap than women? Were you outraged by the news as you were with the gender gap, or were you skeptical?

Were you upset with my opinion that confidence is a choice, and to do better in the working world, short men need more of it?

I'm guessing you didn't think much of the height wage gap, and your reaction was maybe a shrug of the shoulders.

You then bought ten additional copies of this book so you could use them as fire starters and curse my name every time you lit one up.

I base these assumptions on the reactions I received from people who critiqued that chapter for me. I intentionally sought out others with different opinions to gauge the responses. While none of them went as far as telling me to check my white male privilege, they were upset with my opinions. Yet when they learned there was a similar height wage gap, they were mostly silent.

Why does one pay discrepancy cause so much turmoil, and another is met with silence? If you believe one pay discrepancy is due to discrimination, wouldn't it stand to reason the other is as well?

On the other hand, if you agree with me that the gender wage gap is due mostly to women's choices, you enjoyed that chapter because it served as a confirmation bias to you. It felt good to read such a reasonable and well-thought-out case to disprove the discrimination angle. You read the links, which served as additional confirmation for what you already believed.

In fact, you bought ten additional copies of this book to give to friends and family because it's so damn reasonable you think everybody should know about it.[173]

But even if you disagree with me, what does it matter? Why does a different opinion upset so many people these days?

---

173   And I thank you for that. No need to stop at ten, though.

I truly believe it's a result of our volatile political climate. We're being conditioned to think people with different opinions, especially political ones, have bad intentions.

Don't believe me? Turn on any cable news channel or listen to any political pundit's podcast or radio show.

Their mind-reading abilities are astounding, aren't they? They impute negative intent on their political enemies at every opportunity and assume the people on their side are virtuous.

Let us not forget, violent criminals think themselves virtuous as well.[174]

If you're a lefty, you're generally outraged when anyone on Fox News makes these assumptions. If you're a righty, you're generally outraged when anyone on CNN or MSNBC makes the same type of assumptions.

We don't watch the news these days to get the news. We watch the news these days so others can tell us what to think, or, at the very least, to help reinforce what we already believe.

We want others to know that we have good intentions, yet we're not willing to extend the same courtesy to those we disagree with. When we impute negative intent on the enemy, it becomes easy to demonize them. Demonization leads to hate. Hate leads to a fragmented society where we recoil into our little tribes and create our own echo chambers that shield us from opposing views. Societal relationships worsen from there.

We're trying to survive a belly flop from a one-hundred-foot drop.[175] Unless we alter how we're going to enter the water, we're done for.

---

174 Dana Goldstein, "Can Violence Be Virtuous?" *The Marshall Project,* February 12, 2015, https://www.themarshallproject.org/2015/02/12/can-violence-be-virtuous
175 Fuzzy & Nutz, "What If You Belly Flop From 100 Feet (30 meters)?" Published on July 12, 2018, Video, 3:01, https://www.youtube.com/watch?v=ZndOdQ3L1QU

Here's a little secret: This book did not turn out the way I thought it would. Part of the reason is because I've learned a lot in the two years since I started this project.

I'd say this is roughly 30 percent about heightism, and the rest is social commentary on the dangers of the victim mentality, identity politics, and the righteous movement to destroy Buzzfeed.[176]

I guess you can say I fell short of my original goal of making a book mainly about heightism.[177]

This started as a call to short men to unite and fight for the rights given to all other marginalized groups except us. I wanted to change society to see us more favorably and treat us equally. I wanted to show you how much hate we receive on social media. I wanted to plead my case using facts and data and logic.

After reading the first draft, I was embarrassed. During the initial excitement of starting a project on a topic I was passionate about, I realized it was dripping with victimhood mentality and hypocrisy. I was advocating for starting a movement based on tactics that, if another group implemented them, I would ignore and mock.

I was simultaneously encouraging short men to unite and use their VM to march for their rights while at the same time encouraging people to get out of the VM.

So my project changed drastically.

It was at this time the universe smiled upon me. I started researching such topics as identity politics and systemic discrimination. I stumbled across a YouTube video of some dude named Dave Rubin who was interviewing conservative pundit Larry Elder.[178] If you can free up an hour of your time, it's well worth the watch.

---

176   #Buzzfeedcaneatshitanddie
177   That's a short joke. Bada bing!
178   The Rubin Report, "Larry Elder and Dave Rubin: Conservatives, Black Lives Matter, Racism," Published on January 15, 2016, Video, 1:01:14, https://www.youtube.com/

Though I thoroughly enjoyed the interview, the thing that impressed me was Rubin admitting very shortly afterward that this was a seminal moment in his life. Elder basically shattered Rubin's preconceived notion that systemic racism was a problem in America.

Instead of editing the video and discounting what Elder told him, Rubin aired the video without edits and was very open about the fact that Elder changed his mind on the subject.

It's hard to admit that you were wrong, and it's even harder when you're a public figure like Rubin. Yet he did, and that courage is why I'm a huge fan of him to this day.

That video changed my life, too, though in a different way. As a result of my man crush on Rubin, I found out about Ben Shapiro, Joe Rogan, Sam Harris, Jordan Peterson, Christina Hoff Sommers, Cassie Jaye, and the list goes on.

Maybe you've heard of it, but many of these people comprise what is known as the Intellectual Dark Web. They seek out individuals with different opinions and debate and openly deliberate on hard-to-discuss topics. They do it in a respectful way, without ad hominem attacks and with an open mind. They have difficult conversations with people they disagree with instead of demonizing them and shutting them out.

It's the sort of discourse we need. Running and hiding from other opinions and imputing negative intent onto others is cowardly.

Don't be a coward.

As I said in the beginning, if you disagree with me on the contents of this book, feel free to contact me. I'm willing to listen and consider your opinion and viewpoints. But if you don't do it respectfully, don't expect a response.

watch?v=IFqVNPwsLNo&t=1s

As my book changed, so did my objectives and, consequently, my proposed solutions.

I hope other people in marginalized groups and those who suffer from the VM can learn something from all this. After all, I've been there. From what I've observed, people with the VM tend to act out in similar ways, and those who choose to play victims do so for a lot of the same reasons as others. So while I can do my best to empathize with their lived experiences, there's no way for me to know exactly what they've been through. My criticisms of those with the VM are coming from a place of familiarity and empathy, and I hope to reach those people with some solutions that are working for me.

Give my suggestions a shot. Worst-case scenario is you'll end up a better person.

Change yourself and confront your own biases before demanding others to change and confront their biases.

My endgame begins with me and short men in general.

I realize if I want to be treated equally, I must earn it.

It's not fair for me to demand others to see me differently if I'm not willing to prove I deserve it.

If people were judging me when I had the VM, it probably wasn't because I was short. I don't think strangers wander around every day consciously judging others based on their physical characteristics. If it happened, it was probably because I had an air of negativity and cynicism about me, *worried* that others were judging me. And because I was worried that others were judging me, I was doing the same to them.

I felt it was important for others to treat me with the respect I thought I deserved, even when I was strutting around with the stereotypical, angry, short-man attitude. Of course, that's a two-way street: you only get it if you give it, and I wasn't willing to give it.

It took a long time to figure out I had to change myself and the way I treated others to change others' perceptions about me. And with those changes, it gives others less of a reason to negatively stereotype me.

I used my personal powers to influence the way others perceive me.

For me it was an attitude change. For some, it could be as simple as changing the clothes they wear. Buzzfeed's Pedro Fequiere proved that to himself.[179]

This is not earthquake-inducing news. It's why we dress up for job interviews, weddings, church, dates, nights out on the town with friends, etc.

Yet many, like Pedro, refuse to use their personal powers to garner more respect in society. Even though he wants to feel more comfortable in public and claims to fear for his life because of his appearance, he says, "But I won't conform and change my appearance just to make people feel more comfortable around me."

If Pedro is unwilling to make positive changes in his life that will prompt others to judge him more favorably, why should others be willing to see him more favorably?

Pedro's on a mental one-way street. It's a selfish, "everybody has to change to accept me for who I am" mentality.

Life doesn't work that way. It will never work that way.

Changing your wardrobe is crucial for short men as well. It's important to find clothes that fit properly or to get your new digs tailored. If you aren't willing to take the time to do that, people will notice. You may

---

179 #Buzzfeedcaneatshitanddie

end up looking childish, sloppy, and unkempt, and that helps perpetuate the notion that maybe the Randy Moss commercial mentioned earlier is correct: Short adult men are nothing but older children, unable to take care of themselves, and aren't able to look presentable in public. You're not doing yourself or other short men any favors.

My point is, be better than Pedro. Don't choose to be a victim. Take personal responsibility for what you can. When you do that, others will equate what you do, how you look, and how you act to other short men.

By acting accordingly, you can help shatter people's prejudices against us.

This isn't a radical or controversial idea. We all know people who don't fit the stereotype of their group. It makes it harder to pigeonhole the rest of them as a result.

So reform yourself. It will help people realize that judging individuals based on their immutable characteristics or tribe is ignorant. Then we can get to a place where we judge people based on the content of their character, not on their physical characteristics.

Hey, this short man has a dream, too.

FYI, MLK Jr. was only five foot seven.

If you can't (or won't) change something about yourself, don't expect others to change to appease you.

We must learn to listen to each other.

Let's start out with this premise: The person I disagree with wants what's best for humanity just like I do, but he or she has a different way to go about it.

Instead of hating them for having different thoughts and opinions, understand they have good intentions like you. You'll be astonished at how this very simple change in mentality can alter the way you view humankind. The second you start implementing that, your life will get exponentially better.[180]

Darryl Davis is a black musician who has a unique hobby. He befriends members of the Ku Klux Klan, and many of them quit the KKK as a result. The documentary *Accidental Courtesy* is about his endeavors.

His story highlights how effective an individual can be when it comes to changing people's minds about others. Simply put, Darryl and the people he befriends sit down and talk about their differences because, as he puts it, everyone just wants to be heard.

When they leave the hate group, they often give Darryl their Klan robes. He has about twenty-five robes from former members who have quit because of their friendship with him.

Like me, Darryl has an endgame: "My endgame is to bring people together."

He's one man making a positive difference. No screaming. No bull-horns. No demanding anything from the other person.

In 2017, a Black Lives Matter group showed up at a pro-Trump rally to counter protest. You've seen this scenario play out plenty since Trump was elected.

But this time, instead of just the general hatred, yelling, and violence that always occurs, Hawk Newsome, the leader of Black Lives Matter New York, was invited to speak on stage. And the damnedest thing happened: He spoke, his enemies listened, and they found out they have a lot more in common than they ever knew.

Newsome said this about the experience:

It kind of restored my faith in some of those people, because

---

180   Don't believe me? How about you try it. I triple-dog dare you.

when I spoke truths, they agreed.

I feel like we made progress. I feel like two sides that never listen to each other actually made progress today. Did I expect to go on stage? No. I expected to come down here with my fist in the air in a very militant way, exchange insults, maybe some dirty looks, or who knows what. If not on a grander level, but just person to person, I think we really made some substantial steps, without either side yielding anything.

I hope they understand that one of the leaders of the Black Lives Matter movement is a proud American and a Christian, who cares deeply about the country and the people in it, whether they are documented or not. I want them to understand that we are educated, that we apply strategy, but we come from a place of love. We really are here to help this country move towards a better place, not to destroy it.

We came out, we were gonna chant, we were gonna do a demonstration, but we didn't have to. We just spoke. It worked. I'm happy about that.[181]

Comedian Sarah Silverman made headlines in late 2017 when she gave an interview promoting her new television series, *I Love You, America*:

When you're one-on-one with someone who doesn't agree with you, or whose ideology is different than yours, when you're face-to-face, your porcupine needles go down. The surprise was … I fell in love with them [Trump supporters]. I had a great time with them, and I felt comfortable.

I'm finding if I do engage with someone who is angry at me,

---

181 "Trump Supporters Allow Freedom of Speech for #BlackLivesMatter On Stage At MOAR Rally," Published on September 21, 2017, Video, 6:45, https://www.youtube.com/watch?v=3tWPMbQ_PCA

or angry, and I'm a place where they can put that anger … it's almost always a good experience because more than anything, all of us what we have in common is, we want to feel seen. We want to feel like we exist. We really should – all of us – work on not getting our self-esteem from outside forces, but it is so much when somebody just sees you. It's just like, everything melts away. We just all just human out again.[182]

If we can all let go of our bigoted prejudices and start acting like decent human beings to one another, we can put a dent in discrimination faster than you can imagine. But this takes skills in communicating, specifically in listening.

Steven Covey, author of the book *The 7 Habits of Highly Effective People*, said, "Most of us don't listen with the intent to understand. We listen with the intent to reply."[183]

Cassie Jaye says it beautifully in her aforementioned TedxMarin speech:

And there's an important rule in documentary filmmaking. As an interviewer, you do not interrupt. So I'm asking questions, and I'm getting their full life story, and in the moment, I didn't realize it, but now looking back I can see, that while I was conducting my interviews, I wasn't actually listening. I was hearing them speak, and I knew the cameras were recording, but in those moments of sitting across from my enemy, I wasn't listening.

What was I doing? I was anticipating. I was waiting to hear a sentence, or even just a couple of words in succession, that proved what I wanted to believe. That I had found the misogynists. The ground zero of the war on women …

182 Jenna Amatulli, "Sarah Silverman Says She 'Fell In Love' With Trump Voters While Traveling," *Huffington Post,* November 21, 2017, https://www.huffingtonpost.com/entry/sarah-silverman-says-she-fell-in-love-with-trump-voters-while-traveling_us_5a146581e4b03dec82488ccb
183 Stephen R. Covey, "Using Empathic Listening to Collaborate," *Trans4Mind,* 1989, https://trans-4mind.com/counterpoint/index-communication-relationships/covey.shtml

In looking back on the 37 diaries I recorded that year, there was a common theme: I would often hear an innocent and valid point that a men's rights activist would make, but in my head I would add on their statement a sexist or anti-woman spin, assuming that's what they wanted to say but didn't ...

An MRA would say to me, "Men are roughly 78 percent of all suicides throughout the world." And I would counter with, "But women attempt suicide more often, so HA!" Ha? It's not a contest, but I kept making it into one. Why couldn't I simply learn about men's issues and have compassion for male victims without jumping at the opportunity to insist that women are the real victims?

Before making the Red Pill movie, I was a feminist of about 10 years, and I thought I was well-versed on gender equality issues. But it wasn't until I met men's rights activists that I finally started to consider the other side of the gender equality equation. It doesn't mean that I agreed with all that they said. But I saw the immense value in listening to them and trying to see the world through their eyes. I thought if I could get my audience to also listen to them, it could serve as a rung on the ladder, bringing us all up to a higher consciousness about gender equality ...

If I could give advice to anyone in our society at large: We have to stop expecting to be offended, and we have to start truly, openly and sincerely, listening. That will lead to a greater understanding of ourselves and others. Having compassion for one another. Working together toward solutions, because we all are in this together. And once we do that, we can finally heal from the inside out.

But it has to start with listening.[184]

A prime example of not listening is the Cathy Newman interview of Jordan Peterson from early 2018 on Britain's Channel 4. During the entire thirty-minute interview, Newman mischaracterized most of what Peterson said.

At one point during the discussion about the gender wage gap, Peterson called her out for not listening: "I didn't say that at all. That's because you're actually not listening. You're just projecting." To which Newman said, "I am listening very carefully, and I am hearing you say women need to just accept that they're never gonna make it on equal terms; equal outcomes is how you defined it." Peterson laughed during her tirade, telling her he thought her projections were "silly."[185]

What's fascinating is Newman believed she was "listening very carefully," when anyone who watched the interview saw her projecting and mischaracterizing far more than she listened.

It should make you a bit uneasy when a professional journalist, someone paid very well for her work, can't distinguish between when she's projecting and when she's listening. If a trained professional can't realize it, how hard is it for the rest of us?

Get the law on our side.

I don't want to see short men with a victim mentality, and the last thing I want to do is to help foster a victim mentality in them. That's why I would be hesitant to be part of any large organization of shorties taking to the streets to fight for equality. I don't think that strategy works like it used to. I think it was effective when people were fighting for inclusion, such as during the civil rights movement. Movements

184 Cassie Jaye, "Meeting The Enemy: A Feminist Comes To Terms With the Men's Rights Movement," Published on October 18, 2017, at TedxMarin, Video, 14:47, https://www.youtube.com/watch?v=3WMuzhQXJoY https://www.youtube.com/watch?v=3WMuzhQXJoY&t=40s

185 Channel 4 News, "Jordan Peterson debate on the gender pay gap, campus protests, and postmodernism," Published on January 16, 2018, Video, 29:55, https://www.youtube.com/watch?v=aMcjxSThD54&t=7s

aren't about inclusion anymore; they're about division and exclusion[186] and special rights.

Besides, because there are short white men, other victim groups would not be happy if we received the same legal rights as they do.

There's a notion, especially in today's victimhood culture, that white men can't be victims. White men have white male privilege. We are the patriarchy. Our biological sex and skin color prevent us from having any real social grievance. If we do have a grievance, it's the patriarchy's fault.

Take a look at a tiny fraction of articles and videos telling us as much: "Dear White People, Please Stop Pretending Reverse Racism Is Real,"[187] "2017 News Year's Resolutions for White Guys,"[188] and "How the Patriarchy Harms Men and Boys, Too."[189]

I left college in 2003 with the understanding that people who look like me (other white people with penises) were the main problem in society. If I left college with those thoughts, I can only imagine what people who don't look like me came away believing.[190]

But I don't have to imagine too hard.

I've discussed the topic of my book with friends and acquaintances. On several occasions I've received similar comments: Do you think it's a good idea to bring up this issue with all the racism and sexism in society today?

Whether they are aware of it or not, it's the classic "hierarchy of oppression" (or the "oppression Olympics") argument. We're

186 https://www.theguardian.com/society/2018/mar/01/how-americas-identity-politics-went-from-inclusion-to-division
187 https://www.vice.com/en_us/article/kwzjvz/dear-white-people-please-stop-pretending-reverse-racism-is-real
188 https://www.youtube.com/watch?v=SBluYsydAVc
189 https://www.huffingtonpost.ca/2017/11/10/patriarchy-men-boys_a_23273251/
190 That rhetoric is worse on college campuses today than it was when I received my undergraduate degree.

bombarded every single day by the news and social media about the evils of racism and sexism. They are the holy grails of "isms." Any other "ism" is child's play. Because there's never a mention of heightism, there's a sense that it can't be that bad, or it barely exists, or it's all in our heads. They're ranking heightism so low on the totem pole of oppression that it's not a worthwhile issue to discuss, let alone write a book about.

Of course, it doesn't help that at least 95 percent of the time when I tell people about heightism, they laugh. It's honestly perplexing to me. I'd never dream of laughing in someone's face if they told me they experienced racism or sexism, yet I'm hesitant to bring up heightism most of the time because of the inevitable initial response from others.

Most people don't realize that allowing us the same federal protections as other marginalized groups doesn't cost them a thing, except a special victim status. If a short guy is denied a job or a promotion because of his height, is it unreasonable to allow him the same legal recourse that people in other marginalized groups have access to? Or should he just deal with it because he has a penis?

Mentioning us in antibullying materials doesn't mean society is turning its back on homosexuals or blacks who may be bullied as well. It just means that fewer short men will be picked on, and they may have better mental health and confidence as a result. Is this an unreasonable request, or do we need to just embrace our male privilege, be happy we don't sleep with someone of the same sex, and pray we don't become suicidal later in life?

Let's be honest here; the vast majority of the country knows they are not supposed to outwardly bully or discriminate against people in federally protected groups. We are reminded of that every single day! We're taught it at home, in elementary school, in middle school, in high school, and in college. We know this from television and movies and the news we watch. We know this from our jobs and careers.

Employers know they aren't legally allowed to pay women or blacks less because of their genitals or the color of their skin, and it's illegal to do it.

And I'm the one being laughed at and told our problems aren't severe enough to warrant a conversation when all I want is to be included in the current conversation to help my fellow short men.

I'm not asking for much.

So what now?

We must do something. While I remain skeptical of some of the tactics, Tanya Osensky says this in her book, *Shortchanged*:

> Changing the status quo takes more than just complaining. Social attitudes are not going to change by themselves; we have to make it happen. Real, lasting impact will require working together as a group, both on a national level and locally in every community, school, and workplace. We should put pressure on all aspects of society to demand change.
>
> The first step is to build awareness. Disrespect toward short people in the media, in the workplace, and in all different types of interpersonal relationships is nothing more than patent bigotry that should be banished from acceptable behavior. It is time to stop pretending that this issue does not exist. There are millions of short people in this country with their own stories to tell about their experience. We should band together and become activists. We should take our stories to the media and force dialogue about the issues that concern us ...
>
> We also should insist on meaningful legal reform. Federal antibullying laws should support victims of bullying regardless of "why" they are being bullied. Federal and state laws should be reviewed and amended to ensure clarity that workplace

discrimination on the basis of height will no longer be tolerated, that all workers deserve equal pay and opportunities for advancement at work. Because height discrimination is so unknown, passing such laws will require pressure both politically and socially.

Achieving equality under the law will take a long time, but in the meantime, we must work collectively to change cultural and social attitudes by speaking out and organizing a movement ...

If we want our children, male or female, white or nonwhite, gay or straight, tall or short, to have equal opportunity to pursue and attain whatever goals they set for themselves, then we must work to combat the stereotypes that hold them back. On this, we must all work together. It is time to evolve beyond our instinctual preference for tallness by focusing on our more highly evolved human traits that are associated with emotional intelligence and maturity. Everyone benefits when we display more altruism, empathy, and equality, the values that we learn with wisdom. Courage to act will lead to greater equality and eventually to cultural transformation that will benefit everyone. According to John Stuart Mill, a nineteenth-century philosopher and the first member of the English Parliament to call for women's suffrage, "Every great movement must experience three stages: ridicule, discussion, adoption." Let's get started.[191]

For me, this is about true equality. Not equality of outcome, but equality of opportunity. It's about not being metaphorically looked down on in society.

———— ♦ ————

191 Tanya Osensky, *Shortchanged: Height Discrimination and Strategies for Social Change.* Lebanon, NH: University Press of New England, 2017.

I'm still learning about all of this, and I'm sure my views and beliefs will continue to mature and evolve over time. That's part of the reason I encourage you to contact me to discuss the contents of this book.

While I am a big proponent of personal development and believe the best way to go about changing society is to change ourselves first, there are things about the realities of heightism that society needs to know so we can eradicate it from our lives.

Short people are disadvantaged from the beginning, so it's important that children are finally taught that bullying short people is wrong, just like it's wrong to bully people in the federally protected groups.

The media must be aware that the stereotypical and often rotten way they treat us helps perpetuate the negative views that society has of us.

Women should be aware that stating anti-short-man preferences is the same as men stating anti-fat-women preferences, which they are obviously opposed to because the body positivity movement today is still centered around fat women. If you expect us not to be misogynistic pigs against fat women, we expect you not to be misandrist slum dogs toward short men. Fair enough?

Society should be aware and sensitive to the fact that many of us have mental health issues because of the discrimination we face. Suicide could be a bigger problem in the short-man community than in any other group, and we should do our best to prevent that sort of tragedy.

The faster we can bring adequate awareness about heightism to the masses, the faster we can eliminate it and, ideally, other forms of discrimination as well.

Your job is to act accordingly, which includes assuming positive intent of those you disagree with, acting the way you want and expect others to, and holding yourself to the same standards you expect from them. Once we all do that, we'll see a noticeable decrease of discrimination in this country.[192]

I look forward to claiming my place at the table to help end unjust discrimination and make this world a better place to live for all of us.

---

192 Give it a shot. I triple-dog dare you.

Acknowledgments

I would like to thank a few people who were generous with their time by providing feedback on the contents of this book.

The opinions and conclusions in this book are mine. They in no way represent the views of the amazing people who assisted me. I intentionally sought out others with different opinions to help strengthen the content. Unfortunately, in today's political climate, many will equate their assistance with endorsement, and that is not the case. In fact, I can assure you many disagreed with me on much of what I wrote.

To the following people, I am forever grateful (as well as to those who did not want me to mention them):

Seth Ulinski, author of *Amazing Heights: How Short Guys Stand Tall*.

Tanya Osensky, author of *Shortchanged: Height Discrimination and Strategies for Social Change*.

Jessica Ramondi.

Diane Anderson.

Elena Santamaria.

I'd also like to thank all friends and family who have supported me over the past couple years as I follow my dream of being a writer for a living.

And of course, special thanks to Marcy Moo, my Tibetan spaniel, for being the ultimate trooper.

CPSIA information can be obtained
at www.ICGtesting.com
Printed in the USA
BVHW071119060519
547457BV00004B/614/P